1000 Best

Secrets for Your Perfect Wedding

1000 Best

Secrets for Your Perfect Wedding

Sharon Naylor

SOURCEBOOKS, INC.
NAPERVILLE, ILLINOIS

Published by Sourcebooks, Inc.
P.O. Box 4410, Naperville, Illinois 60567-4410
(630) 961-3900
fax: (630) 961-2168
www.sourcebooks.com

Library of Congress Cataloging-in-Publication Data
Naylor, Sharon.
  1000 best secrets for your perfect wedding / by Sharon
Naylor.
    p. cm.
  ISBN 1-4022-0271-7 (alk. paper)
  1. Weddings--Planning. 2. Wedding etiquette. I. Title:
One thousand best secrets for your perfect wedding. II.
Title.
HQ745.N3867 2004
395.2'2--dc22

                            2004012239

              Printed and bound in Canada
              WC 10 9 8 7 6 5 4 3 2

For Madison and Kevin

Table of Contents

PART FIVE: Additional Details

Acknowledgments

A great big thank you to my editors at Sourcebooks, Deborah Werksman and Kelly Barrales-Saylor, for years of effort in creating projects that we can share with you…and also to my tireless and fearless agent Meredith Bernstein for always coming through for me. What a great team!

Many, many thanks to my family and my closest of friends, my writer's community at the American Society of Journalists and Authors, my wedding industry colleagues at the Association of Bridal Consultants and the International Special Events Society, plus the very valued and very talented wedding experts who shared their advice with me for this book: Leslie Vismara of Vismara Invitations, David Walzog and Chris Diviney from the Westminster Hotel, Brenda K. Maynard from Party Plus, Sarah Stitham from Charmed Places, Dana Smith Acosta from Charming Favors, Casey Cooper from Botanicals in Chicago, Rich Penrose from Dean Michaels Studio, and, of course, the fabulous Crys Stewart from *WeddingBells* magazine and her amazing publicist Julie Berry, who always delivers the finest in wedding resources when I call.

Quick! What's the one thing you want your wedding to be? Beautiful? Elegant? Romantic? Very *you?* You might choose *all* of these descriptions for the wedding of your dreams, but the one thing you undoubtedly have planned is for your wedding to be very, very special. Welcome to the book that's going to help you create your big day in the most personalized way possible.

Everything needs to be mapped out and detailed—your ceremony, reception, and all the events immediately before and after—and *you're* in complete control of it all. Don't get overwhelmed at that prospect, though. Yes, it does feel like a ton of work to do in a short period of time, and right now it may seem like there are a thousand little details to be attended to. But the good news is…they're *your* details to handle! This entire wedding is yours to dream up and do. And what you might not be aware of yet is that you're getting married in the best era *ever* for brides and grooms.

Today you can have whatever you want. Gone are the old rules about what's proper and "acceptable" for a formal wedding. Gone are the societal eyebrow raises over theme weddings and brides who dare to wear anything other than a virginal white wedding gown. Gone are the days when your parents paid for the entire wedding and made all the decisions for it. Cookie-cutter weddings…gone. "What will people think?"…gone. "I can't do that because…" That's gone too. You have so much free-dom now to make the wedding of your dreams happen, to completely personalize your day, to mix in your heritage and several religious faiths, to wear a pink gown if you want to, and to ride off after your reception in a hot red convertible instead of a tra-ditional white limousine.

It all starts right now. Get ready to have some fun.

What's Going on in the World of Weddings

The one thing that nearly all brides-to-be have in common is that they want to know what's going on out there in the world of wedding planning. They want to know what other brides and grooms are doing. Not to follow their lead or stick with some safe formula for wedding planning, but for inspira-tion and great ideas to incorporate into our own dreams. That's why we all read the special celebrity wedding editions of our favorite magazines and watch the *Lifetime* celebrity wedding programs. That's why we tune in to *A Wedding Story* on TLC and why we check out the message boards at the top bridal magazine websites.

Speaking of top bridal magazines, Crys Stewart, editor-in-chief of *WeddingBells* magazine and a partner at WeddingChannel.com, very generously allowed me to share with you their latest reader sur-vey responses in order to give you an idea of what's happening among your wedding-planning peers. I've provided some overview statistics here to get you started, and I'll give you more throughout this book. So keep an eye out for the special *Wedding-Bells* survey features on the following pages.

About the Engagement

- 67 percent reported that their engagement took place on "no particularly significant day—just out of the blue"
- 15 percent reported that their engagement took place on a calendar holiday, such as Thanksgiving, Christmas, Chanukah, etc.
- 10 percent reported that their engagement took place on either the anniversary of their first date or their first meeting
- 5 percent reported that their engagement took place on a birthday
- 4 percent reported that their engagement took place on Valentine's Day

About the Wedding

- $27,000 is the average wedding budget reported by all survey respondents
- 81 percent will have a "large wedding"—that is, over one hundred guests
- The average number of guests at receptions is 181
- The average number of guests from out of town is forty-one (Note: Keep this in mind! Having more

out-of-town guests opens up great opportunities for making your wedding weekend special. More on that in later chapters.)

About the Money

To pay for the entire wedding, here's where the survey respondents said they'd go for the cash:

- 17 percent would marry as part of a promotional event, for example, on a television special, as part of a bridal show, etc.
- 12 percent would borrow from family and friends
- 8 percent would max out their credit cards
- 7 percent would take a significant loan
- 3 percent would invest their life's savings
- And then we have the wiser of the wedding couples out there: 66 percent of respondents said "no way" to the above cash sources and would instead maintain a reasonable budget

Wedding Web Cam

- 92 percent of engaged women own a home computer
- 94 percent of engaged women will use the Internet in the planning of their wedding
  (Note: Look at those numbers! Somebody's planning her wedding from the office computer system!)
- 100 percent of engaged women in the survey report having access to the Internet

Who Are These People?

According to the *WeddingBells* survey, their panel of respondents is as follows:

- 100 percent female
- 87 percent of respondents are between the ages of eighteen and thirty-four
- 88 percent are college educated or higher
- The average age of the bride is twenty-seven
- The average age of the groom is twenty-nine
- 72 percent earn over $50,000 a year, with an average income of over $83,000 a year

If those numbers stopped you in your tracks just now, hold on. While it's true that money is a deciding factor in just how much you can dream up for your ideal wedding day, and while many brides and grooms might have a wedding budget that is many times more than what you might be able to afford, don't let the money issue stop you. In this book, you'll get ideas for *all budget ranges*, including low budget, ideas for *free*, and high-budget concepts that you might consider at full price or—creatively—attain for less. I ran the gamut here on price ranges to give you more to consider.

Money is going to be an issue, no doubt about it. Let's be honest about that right up front. But it shouldn't be the biggest issue. What *should* be the biggest issue is finding ways to make your wedding all about the two of you in as many personalized and heartfelt ways as possible. You can't put a price on meaning and sentiment, and some of the most important things about your wedding won't cost a thing at all.

Excited? Good. Let's get started.

PART ONE:

The First Steps

chapter 1

Sharing Your Day

While most wedding books start off asking you what style of wedding you want, how big you want it to be, and whether you're picturing ice sculptures or champagne fountains, a flowing designer gown or a little white slip dress on the beach in Hawaii, I'm taking you to a different starting point, one that reflects a growing trend in brides' and grooms' value systems: *Who do you want to share your wedding with?*

For so many couples, the Where and When aren't as important as the Who. For them, their dream wedding wouldn't be complete without having their entire group of closest friends and family members, the people who really matter to them, there to share every moment. Tell them that they can have a million-dollar wedding at no cost to them, but none of their relatives or friends could come, and they'll undoubtedly say "no thanks."

This is a big thing in the world of weddings today; the importance of sharing your wedding with loved ones and making it a family celebration.

For many reasons (not the least of which is that we live in a post–September 11 world where family togetherness and the gold of friendships are held so much closer to our hearts), it's all about the guest list. We've learned that people are more important than things. And we've shown and seen in our own lives that family is among our highest priorities. So it naturally follows that weddings have followed this phenomenon.

Now, you might be thinking, "But isn't every wedding already planned to include everyone you've ever known, everyone your parents have ever known, and lots of people you don't even know? Aren't guest lists up in the 180s?" Absolutely. Notice I didn't say anything about inviting four hundred people just because you know them. That's the opposite of what I'm saying. What I'm talking about is sharing your wedding day only with people who are special to you. That might mean making your guest list *smaller,* simplifying things all the way around, and truly being able to share your day with the people who are most special to you.

How you interpret and apply that statement is up to you. For you, it could be the huge guest list with all of your college friends, distant relatives, work colleagues, your bosses, your neighbors, and your third grade teacher. Or it might feel better to you to just stick with a close circle of friends and immediate family.

One way this trend has evolved is a *big* change from weddings of past decades, where formal weddings meant no small children were allowed to attend. At $100 per guest for the catering, that's a lot to spend on a four-year-old who will bring her own Lunchables to the dinner and not eat another thing. Now, couples with big family values and a close relationship with their nieces, nephews, and their friends' kids plan weddings where kids are more than welcome. To them, that is what makes it a heart-filled family event. They wouldn't have it any other way, and they plan their weddings accordingly.

1. What matters most is that the people you love and value are there with you on your day. So as you start off at Step 1 by building your guest list, keep this in mind. The names you write create the entire foundation of your wedding plans, since size affects your location and budget.

2. Size does matter. When you're building your initial working guest list, and incorporating all of your parents' and future in-laws' wished-for guests into your master list, the grand total can make your head spin. If you do find yourselves in a position where you simply cannot invite everyone, but wish to cut the list down to the absolute essentials, you can avoid some of the diplomacy headaches by categorizing your list in *tiers*. By this, I mean that your closest family and friends would be Tier 1, second cousins and their families might be Tier 2, distant friends and relatives you haven't seen in a long time might be Tier 3. And with that classification system set, it might be easier to chop names from your list by just removing all Tier 5 people, for instance.

Building Your Inner Circle

No discussion of who to include in your wedding day would be complete without talking about the bridal party. You probably already have some idea who you're going to ask to be your bridesmaids, groomsmen, maid of honor, and best man—or at least you're actively trying to narrow down your long, long list of candidates. Here, I'm going to share some of the newest trends that today's wedding couples are using to make their weddings more special to them.

3. Have *two* best men, if the groom can't select between a brother and a best friend.

4. Have *two* maids of honor (or matrons of honor, if married).

5. The groom can ask his father to be his best man.

6. The bride can ask her mother to be her matron of honor, or even a bridesmaid.

7. Skip the lineup of bridesmaids and grooms-men in favor of just a maid of honor and a best man for simpler, smaller weddings.

8. Have just the best man and maid of honor, and then a collection of adorable, much-loved children in matching flower girl dresses for the girls and mini tuxes for the boys. This is a way to include all of your nieces, nephews, godchildren, the kids you baby-sit for, your students—any children who have a big place in your heart.

9. Make it easy on the guests and participants financially. Since having your favorite people at the wedding is the key, you might choose to generously pick up their expenses (such as wardrobe, travel, and lodging) as a token of appreciation and a big gold star for consideration. Being in a bridal party can be an expensive proposition, so if you're among the couples who can afford to do so, just know that it's completely within the realm of proper behavior to make the offer to your honored bridal party attendants.

Minus the Tuxedo or Bridesmaid's Gown

If you can't fit everyone into your bridal party, as might be the case, you can find positions of honor for your other closest relatives and friends. Your goal is to give them a chance in the spotlight, something important to do or a symbolic role to play, to honor their importance to you. Here are some ideas to get you thinking about status positions for your chosen few.

10. Have each of them read a special passage or psalm during your ceremony.

11. Have them *write* a poem or reading for your ceremony.

12. Have them play a part in an ethnic or religious ritual as a part of the ceremony (such as presenting the host at a Catholic ceremony).

13. Have them perform a song during your ceremony if their great musical talent can be their gift to you.

14. Include in your ceremony a moment of thanks for the couple who introduced you, and present them with roses or a gift.

15. Honor your parents during your ceremony with a special reading, or the offering of roses or a gift.

16. Honor all guests during your ceremony for making the trip to be with you. No need for a rose ceremony, just ask the officiant to read a poem or statement of gratitude from the two of you. (It's so touching when you choose to express thanks to your loved ones during your big "us" moment.)

17. Request that song you and the girls couldn't stop singing during a memorable road trip. Make it all about your bond with all of your closest loved ones, and make memories between you that will last forever.

18. Have them release butterflies or doves at the close of the ceremony.

19. Have them pop the cork on a bottle (or two or three) of champagne immediately after the ceremony for guests to toast the bride and groom. Make the "first cork-popper" a position of honor.

20. At the reception, dedicate special songs or propose toasts to your parents, in-laws, grandparents, the couple or friend who introduced the two of you, anyone who helped with the engagement surprise, siblings, friends who came a long distance to be with you—anyone you'd like to share a moment with.

21. Add on to the lineup of special dances, like the father-daughter dance. There's no rule book for who gets a special dance, and there's no limit if you keep the spotlight dances to just a *portion* of a full song. (Big hint: trade two or three honored partners during the same song.) So dance with your new father-in-law, your grandfather, and the best man.

22. Cue up your Mom's favorite song and twirl with her around the dance floor.

23. Honor any departed relatives or friends during your ceremony with a song, a reading, a moment of remembrance, or simply the dedication of all floral arrangements in their memory. This is a popular trend now, with more and more brides and grooms honoring departed parents, grandparents, godparents, friends, siblings, etc. Don't worry about this being too macabre…it's a wonderful way to feel like a much-missed loved one is more a part of the day. Many brides and grooms report that they were so happy to have a special moment for all guests to remember and say a prayer for their departed loved one. Take a moment right now to list who you'd like to give a spotlight moment to on your wedding day, and what your plan for them will be.

Making Time for People

With a career, a full social schedule, maintaining your relationship with your intended, and the almost inhuman amount of work required to plan a wedding these days, spending quality time with family and friends might seem like a back-burner priority. But it's not. In fact, the time you share with your parents, siblings, and friends while you're in the midst of the wedding whirlwind is very important.

24. Not only will going out for dinner and drinks and a few laughs with your nearest and dearest keep *you* calmer and more rational, it will give all of your relationships a little something special when you're the bride or groom and they're supporting your efforts. It's this time, right now, when your relationships become more important and grow even stronger.

25. Be sure to book those manicure appointments with your best friend, those lunches with your mom, and go see your nephews play in their little league games. Maintaining your own identity and lifestyle will keep you from buckling under the bridal pressure by bringing you back to center and balancing your life. Trust me—you'll need this now more than you'd expect, and enjoying others' company will allow you to make your entire wedding planning process more special. It won't be if you lose yourself in the wedding plans.

chapter 2

Style and Formality

What's your dream wedding style? How does it look? Elegant and formal? Casual and laid-back? Outdoors? On the beach?

Most brides and grooms start off with a picture in their minds. They can see themselves in a grand ballroom, dancing their first dance to the music of a full orchestra. Or they can see themselves on the beach in Jamaica with their maids in floral sundresses and a flower tucked behind the bride's ear. Here's where you'll define your own wedding style, and take it from here to handle all of the details.

It's Just a Formality

One of the biggest factors in a wedding's style is your preference for formality. A traditional, old-fashioned wedding in a ballroom with the five-course dinner and dancing would be formal or ultra-formal. Everything—from the style of gown you'll wear to the menu served to the décor to the invitations you send—hinges on fitting into a formal style (and so does the budget). An outdoor wedding can be highly formal—a veritable Four Seasons ballroom created in the open air—or it can be less formal, in the manner of a family beach party with no one wearing shoes. Any style of wedding can be done with any formality—just keep that in mind. It's the details that make it work.

For now, we're establishing the parameters of your wedding details. We're defining your wedding vision and just how grand—or simple—you want everything to be. In this section, I'll provide some descriptions of real weddings that took place in a variety of styles, with a nod or two to the growing trends in special wedding styles and themes.

26. The *Traditional Formal Evening Wedding* is the model of elegant everything, from a vast array of foods at the cocktail hour, a gourmet dinner, fine décor, good china and crystal on the tables, a several-tiered cake, and dancing throughout the reception. It's the princess wedding for a princess bride—and it's also the model that the $27,000 national average wedding budget figure most often portrays. For many couples, this can be the wedding they want to *escape,* in order to have something different, something more special to them.

27. The *Formal Daytime Wedding* is almost identical to the evening wedding, except it might take place in the afternoon. Everything else is the same.

28. The *Cocktail Party Wedding* is one of those growing trends in wedding styles, where the entire reception is a cocktail party with a lavish buffet of appetizers, carving stations, and gourmet dishes, with the addition of passed *hors d'oeuvres* served by waiters. A cake is cut at the end of the reception, and there may still be dancing at this reception. Couples on a budget who still want an elegant, formal wedding choose this style for its cosmopolitan flair, its more-than-ample menu, and its departure from the more traditional sit-down dinner style of a full reception.

29. The *Dessert and Champagne Wedding* takes place after 8 PM, and the style is formal, chic, and even relaxed. Champagne and fine wines may be served, along with espresso and coffee, plus a menu of cake and delectable desserts like crème brûlée, bananas flambé, chocolate mousse cups, tiramisu, and chocolate-dipped strawberries. Savvy couples with a unique style love this wedding, since it gives their guests a completely new wedding experience, rather than a carbon copy of every other wedding they've been to that season. Plus it's easier on the checkbook. The real allure of this reception is its decadent style—couples tell me they found a great winery or lounge, jazz club or hotel ballroom with elegant couches and 1930s-style décor to make the atmosphere work for this style of wedding. To see more on the style, visit www.westminsterhotel.com for a look at what I picture when I choose a site for a champagne and dessert wedding, just to give you the visual.

30. The *Outdoor Wedding* will always be a romantic fantasy-turned-reality for couples who wish to marry under a tent, out in the open air, on the beach, in a garden, or on a boat. The style may be formal, or it may be less formal, but the key is the beauty of the surroundings. Countless celebrities have held outdoor weddings (helicopters or not), as the essence of a truly romantic and beautiful wedding celebration.

31. The *Mixed-Style Wedding* is another of the big, hot trends in making weddings more special. Wedding coordinator Sarah Stitham at www.charmedplaces.com specializes in finding great rustic locales for weddings, and turning an oversized barn on a gorgeous wooded property into a five-star ballroom by bringing in fine china and linens, using color, and ordering up a sumptuous menu. You, too, can mix styles like this, giving your guests a big surprise and a truly special wedding that makes full use of a site's grounds, walkways, scenic vistas, and great photo opportunities.

32. The *Ethnic Wedding* is on the rise, thanks to movies like *My Big Fat Greek Wedding*, and also thanks to the "family is everything" values trend, where couples are embracing more of their heritage and their families' core belief systems. As modern as a couple might be, they may feel strongly that they want the same cultural rituals their parents (or grandparents or ancestors) performed at their weddings woven into twenty-first-century celebrations. So you might see a traditional Korean wedding ceremony with the bride in full Korean garb, followed by a more Western reception where the bride changes into a traditional wedding gown, with many Korean menu options, musical accompaniment, and décor options mixed in.

33. The *Multi-Cultural Wedding* and the *Interfaith Wedding* blends the two worlds of the bride and groom with a customized mix of each partner's most valued beliefs and practices. Often, modern couples spend a great deal of time researching traditional wedding customs and celebrations to include, even reaching out to their heritage's national association and ethnic websites for help, or sitting before a faith officiant who can instruct them on details of wedding rites that might not have been seen in their families for two generations. We're a culture embracing our roots more than ever, and the inclusive wedding of today brings more cultural accents into a wedding as a tribute to the bride, groom, and family. This, too, makes a wedding extra special, as a unique experience for guests who have been to too many bland, cookie-cutter weddings.

34.

The *Traveling Wedding* is a trend that's been hot in the South for a long time and is spreading across the country and the world. Rather than the usual cocktail hour followed by a formal dinner, the traveling wedding sets up "stations" at several sites on a property's grounds. At the first stop, your guests might gather at poolside for passed *hors d'oeuvres* and tropical drinks. Then everyone moves on to a decorated terrace for margaritas and a fully stocked seafood bar. Next, the crowd moves on to an indoor party room where dinner is served, and then everyone goes back out to poolside for dessert and after-dinner drinks. What is served—the theme of each offering—at each stop is up to you, but the style of wedding again gives guests a unique experience with surprises at every turn, and plenty of mingling time while they're in transit. When considering wedding locations, look at a great site for its adaptability to this traveling wedding style—a poolside area with tables, a terrace, a lounge, a formal dining area, and a cigar or piano bar all suggest great places for each stop on your wedding journey.

35. The *Theme Wedding* has come a long way from the times when "theme party" had you cringing and hoping you weren't going to wind up wearing any kind of hokey costume. Now theme weddings are incredibly elegant and imaginative, unique, and most welcome to guests who want that unique experience along with you. Here are some of the most popular theme weddings that have been done with style, class, and originality:

• Winter Wonderland
• An Evening in Tuscany
• A Midsummer Night's Dream (like the Shakespearean play, this one takes place in a wooded or tree-encircled area with great views of the sky and a magical element to it)
• Under the Stars
• Under the Sea
• Mardi Gras
• 1920s to 1930s speakeasy style
• Halloween (*very* popular for its fun factor and décor possibilities—also held in a nonpeak wedding month so prices may be lower!)

The options go on and on, but it's always the couple using an element of their personalities and favorite things, a favorite holiday or season, or something else that's very *them* that makes an elegant theme wedding more attractive to them—and perhaps to you as well. Just be sure that you or your wedding coordinator knows that subtlety is best, because a theme *can* be taken too far. Choose wisely.

36. The *Destination Wedding* is one of the biggest trends we're seeing today, with couples flying off—along with two dozen of their closest friends and family—to an island or international resort where the wedding will be held. The lure of a travel adventure is unmistakable, since getting married during a Hawaiian sunset is the ideal in romance, and such destinations offer amazing adventures for all wedding guests. Where else could you fill your wedding weekend with swimming with dolphins, scuba diving, taking a canopy tour of rainforests, or touring Mayan ruins? This vacation getaway is perfect for travelers and adventure-seekers, and perhaps for brides and grooms who want to just get away from it all with a select group of revelers—and let the resort coordinators do all of the hard planning work.

37. A subset of the destination wedding is the *Mini Destination Wedding*, where you're not flying off to an island in the Caribbean or to the Riviera, but instead traveling three to four hours from home to a resort that's just a short hop away— no passports required. This is a big one right now, with more couples wanting to get out of the crowded and expensive big cities where they live to the nearby mountains and lake areas where they have wineries and horseback riding at their disposal. The wedding party can take over a bed-and-breakfast establishment, a family-style lodge by a golf course, or discover some of the truly great resort-and-spa destinations just outside your area. The destination might not be far away, but it does open a new world of possibilities.

We'll talk more about great locations in Chapter 4, but I wanted to get you primed and thinking about the style of wedding you want. Once you have that picture in your mind, the rest falls into place and you can build your special wedding plans from there.

chapter 3

Setting the Date

Another big building block that can affect the look, feel, style, and—of course—cost of your wedding is the date on which you hold it. There's a vast difference between the kind of wedding you can hold in June and the one in the snowy winter months. Summer brings the options of beach weddings and outdoor receptions. Winter holiday months can give you an ice crystal wonderland with red poinsettias, evergreens, and gently falling snow as the backdrop for your pictures.

The date you choose depends heavily on the season you favor.

38. Think about prices. You've undoubtedly heard about prices for weddings being higher in some months than in others, and that's absolutely true. It used to be that May through August was the peak wedding season, with wedding experts and reception halls hiking up their prices to meet supply and demand. Now September and October join those months as the so-called peak wedding season. Obviously, those months all give you a great chance at beautiful weather for your big day, which is why they are so popular. Brides and grooms on a budget might like hearing that the wedding industry generally drops their prices in January, but who wants to risk facing a major snowstorm on their wedding day? Indeed, it is a trade-off to keep in mind, but please remember the rainy seasons we've had the past few summers. And think about some beautiful weather you may have experienced in November where you live. The weather should never be a deciding factor in the date you choose for your wedding, as Mother Nature isn't held to any boundaries. No one is guaranteed a gorgeous day, no matter which block on the calendar they choose.

39. The bigger issue is which season fits the style of wedding you have in mind? You might be a traditionalist and wish to be a June bride, or you might be one of those who just love the autumn months. Maybe you'd rather marry in the fall when the leaves are in full, passionate color on the trees. Or possibly your wedding dream has you all at a luxurious ski resort in the height of winter. Look at your wedding image and then think of the season that works for you.

It's All in the Timing

40. Allow enough time to plan. The most important factor when choosing any wedding date is giving yourselves enough time to plan the wedding. With your busy schedule, and with local churches and reception halls fully booked for all weekends in the coming months, it might be wiser to give yourselves at least a year's time before your wedding date arrives.

41. Allowing plenty of months in preparation time gives you more options, and it also allows you a less stressful planning period during which you don't have to rush, don't have to take a hasty offer due to that loudly ticking clock (not *that* clock, the other one!).

42. If time is not a problem for you, you *can* plan your wedding in less than a year. So look six months down the road and see if it is possible for you and your intended to carry out your plans with little hassle. While it may seem like everyone is spending eighteen months planning their weddings, yours could arrive much sooner.

Steer Clear of Mother's Day!

43. Yes, it is true. Flowers—particularly roses—are going to be more expensive during the time of Mother's Day and Valentine's Day. It's just a fact of the floral industry, one of those supply and demand issues that hits any consumer at certain times of the year.

44. Planning your wedding to coincide with a holiday weekend *could* be a wise move on your part. Wedding planners, hotel event managers, florists, and photographers all say that certain holidays are on many engaged couples' wish lists. Why the spotlight sharing? For many, holidays are a time when their family and friends will already be in town. It's tremendously convenient for wedding guests to make one cross-country flight back home than two. Remember, weddings now are all about who you want to share them with, so choosing Thanksgiving weekend for your wedding date might be a welcome announcement to many. Especially since going to *your* wedding means they won't be able to make it to their in-laws' house this year!

45. Another issue that makes holiday times so popular for weddings is the *party factor*. Having a New Year's Eve wedding adds something extra special to your late-night reception when the countdown begins, the confetti flies, and a brand new year coincides with the start of your marriage.

46. Getting romantic, Valentine's Day has been and always will be a top choice for wedding dates, especially for couples who got engaged on Valentine's Day.

Other Holiday Wedding Choices

47. Mardi Gras is a great time to celebrate— mix up some Hurricanes and get those colorful bead necklaces out for a party worthy of Bourbon Street.

48. Halloween may be low on popularity lists for weddings—making it great timing for availability and often great pricing. It also bring out your playful side by asking guests to come in costume, adding a unique element of fun to your day.

49. Despite travel hassles, Memorial Day weekend or Labor Day weekend are a three- to four-day weekend for everyone.

Personal Holidays

50. Marry on the anniversary of the date he proposed to you, and that's an instant swoon and a blush of romance.

51. Marry on your birthday, and it's twice the celebration.

52. Marry on the anniversary of your first date, and that's just poetry and a fairy-tale ending.

53. Marry on your parents' or grandparents' anniversary, and it's an honor to their partnerships as well as perhaps a good luck charm to you.

A Warning About Wedding Dates

54. Be sure that your wedding date won't coincide with any religious or cultural holidays that restrict guests' diets. During the month of Lent, for example, many of your guests might not be permitted to eat meat during your Friday evening reception. That's an unwelcome surprise if you've spent a fortune on filet mignon, prime rib, or other meat dishes for your dinner. It's something to be aware of, ask about, and plan for.

Do You Have the Time?

The next factor is the time of day at which your wedding will be held. The standards of formality have stated in the past that formal weddings should be held in the late afternoon to early evening, dessert weddings are later in the evening, and luncheons and cocktail parties are in the afternoon. This traditional list still holds true today. Hold your wedding at dinnertime, and guests should get a dinner. Marry in the morning, and your guests get breakfast, brunch, or lunch.

55. It's the time on the clock that dictates the style and possibilities for your entire wedding day. So what's the best time for a truly special wedding? Anytime.

56. Morning weddings are picking up steam, with brunches and luncheons rising in the ranks of wedding styles.

57. Those late-night dessert and champagne receptions are gaining in popularity as well.

58. And then you have the sunset weddings—timed to coincide with an amazing, beautifully colored sunset over the water or the mountains. Time your ceremony for the exact moment the sun starts to sink into the horizon, filling the sky with oranges, reds, corals, and purples, and that's a truly special way to make your wedding something spectacular. So how do you time your wedding for sunset when you're talking about a date that's months in advance? Simple. Go to http://aa.usno.navy.mil and click on their precise sunset timer for any day of the year. As for the extraordinary sunset before you, you can't pay for that kind of backdrop to your wedding day.

chapter 4

Location is Everything

By far, one of the most important first decisions you'll make that can set the entire stage for your beautiful, unique, and special wedding is the location or locations at which your wedding will take place.

59. Take every element of a traditional wedding in a church or synagogue and then at a reception hall, and—as breathtaking as they might be—transport them in your mind to a botanical garden or a winery. The new, out-of-the-ordinary setting can make every one of those same plans just a bit more special with the added allure of a unique location and all of its unrivaled ambience.

60. Make no mistake, I'm *not* saying that a traditional wedding held in a church and reception hall can't be special. It certainly can, when you choose a lovely atmosphere with all of the dream elements you originally pictured. You can dress up even the most plain ballroom into a stunning scene right out of a movie with the right choice of décor, lighting, table settings, and the many ideas we'll get into in Chapters 17 and 18.

61. Some couples have written in to tell me about how they took a plain hotel ballroom and transformed it into a Moroccan oasis with lush burgundy couches; red, orange, and yellow tapestries; professional belly dancers in performance; tables set with rich gold accents; and music to transport their guests to a magical *Arabian Nights* fantasy. Anything can be done with any space at all. More on that later. For now, let's concentrate on finding unique settings for your wedding based on the appeal of their atmosphere and how *that* will make you and your guests feel to be there.

62. It goes without saying, of course, that when you're looking at any site for your ceremony or reception, you're primarily considering functional aspects such as, "Is it big enough to hold our guests?" or "Is it too cavernous for our smaller, more intimate group?" You must also consider whether it has adequate parking, restroom facilities, air conditioning or heat, handicapped access, and the like. Once these items are checked off as "okay" on your criteria list, the place is up for your inspection.

What Makes a Location Truly Special

Here, I'm listing a selection of qualities that a unique and extra-special location might offer you. These are the attractions you might look for, those incredible sights and accompanying sounds that depart from the cookie-cutter wedding and can have you literally jumping up and down when you finally discover your own dream wedding location after checking out a few dozen other places. Read on and highlight those that make your own wish list.

63.

Winery: Wineries across the country have gotten into the business not just of making great Chablis, Chardonnay, Merlot, and Shiraz, but of hosting amazing parties. Many have elegant tasting rooms with leather couches and libraries, outdoor party areas and dimly lit down-stairs wine cellars where your wedding could take place. And for a fresh-air party, it doesn't get more beautiful and natural than a tent staked on the fresh, fertile earth of a vineyard. Vineyard areas have mass tourist appeal, so you'll undoubtedly find fabulous hotels and bed and breakfasts, shop-ping, hot air balloon rides, bicycle rental stands, farmers' markets, horseback riding...the works. Wineries are now among the top choices of brides and grooms for great wedding locations, so check in your area for the top wineries available, or go to the national meccas of wine country: Napa Valley, Sonoma County, and Mendocino in California (note: that's one great destination wedding choice).

Check It Out

64.

To find wineries and vineyards near you, visit www.winespectator.com for lists and links to all the top-rated wineries in the country and overseas.

65. *Botanical Garden:* The most gorgeous botanical gardens with flowering fields and outdoor wedding sites right out of the pages of a highly styled magazine spread are out there just waiting for your wedding. From fields of colorful tulips to English countryside gardens, tropical gardens complete with waterfalls to butterfly gardens, outside *and* inside gardens, there are gardens for any time of the year. If your dream wedding has you surrounded by the most beautiful flowers, plants, and trees, check out botanical gardens, arboretums, and conservatories near you.

66. *Aquarium:* For that "Under the Sea" feel, with enormous glass walls showing you an underwater wonderland of colorful fish, stingrays, even sharks or dolphins, check out a highly-rated aquarium near you. You might not be aware yet that many aquariums regularly host weddings and big corporate parties, so they may have excellent party areas and even ballrooms ready for your use, caterers on site, and the makings of a terrific theme wedding. Even better, you don't need to spend a dime decorating your wedding site, because it doesn't get better than the oceanic scenes all around you.

67. *Museum:* Great museums are hosting wonderful weddings and elegant corporate parties, bringing your event right up close to their paintings and jewelry displays. Again, these establishments may also have incredible party rooms or ballrooms, and they will certainly be able to guide you to their favorite caterers, cake bakers, florists, and other professionals who know their space and have worked it well in the past. This often overlooked opportunity makes for a unique and special wedding.

68. *Art Gallery:* Even the most modest art gallery is often the site for corporate parties, special promotional events, and weddings. You rent the space for the evening, and the staff transforms the site into your ideally decorated wedding arena. Keep in mind that it's fabulously chic in big cities to have parties at or in conjunction with art galleries, and it's a great choice if you love and support the arts as a couple. This could be a great way to bring your own tastes and values into the mix, creating a wedding that to any of your guests is unquestionably *you*.

69. *Yacht:* Climb aboard an elegantly appointed private yacht, or even one of those big party boats, for a sailing adventure on the water. The scenery slowly passing by might be the bright city lights, a beachfront with lighthouses and dolphins diving ahead of you, or a beautifully-lit marina if you don't choose to sail off into the sunset, but rather remain moored to land. The amazing selection of high-society yachts for hire out there is truly incredible, offering beautiful staterooms, brass railings, leather couches, big time entertainment centers with surround sound, a galley where gourmet chefs can cook up amazing meals for your guests, and the unmistakable ocean air on a cool summer's evening.

70. *Lighthouse:* Today, our national landmarks are being protected, refurbished, and kept in service by a team of volunteers and people who love their historical monuments. That said, you should know that many lighthouses welcome visitors, open their buildings and surrounding land to private parties, and offer amazing cliff-side and ocean views. With resorts just down the shoreline, this could be a bright spot in your search for the perfect, unique, and special wedding location.

71. *Bed and Breakfast:* So many bed and breakfasts out there are the very definition of the word "charming." I've seen beautiful Victorian bed and breakfasts in pastel candy colors with Laura Ashley-inspired bedrooms and outdoor terraces lined with rocking chairs and hammocks. Take over one of these establishments for your wedding, and you have the whole "hotel" at your disposal, not to mention the kindly innkeeper who will make you an amazing breakfast or tea time sandwiches.

Finding a Bed and Breakfast

72. To find a charming and lovely bed and breakfast near you, or in a city where you might take a destination wedding, check out www.bedandbreakfast.com.

73. *Orchard:* Set up your tables, chairs, and picnic blankets out in the lush fields of an orchard for an open-air wedding to remember. The fruit-filled trees provide the décor and the aroma, and along with some great decorating choices, you can transform that field into an amazing wedding location. Some orchards provide hayrides for the kids, fruit picking, farmers' stands, and hay mazes for family outings and more playful, informal weddings.

74. *Mansion or Estate Home:* Check with the nearby historical association or chamber of commerce to inquire about mansions or estate homes that regularly rent out their spaces for weddings and big parties. You might have the run of the mansion, using their beautifully decorated common rooms, libraries, lounges, indoor pool areas (perfect for your cocktail party), their gardens and alcoves, outdoor gardens and marble fountains, terraces, and dining rooms for your visit to the fine life.

75. *Refurbished Barn:* As mentioned earlier, one of the newly built, modern architectural masterpiece barns can be your dream location with a terrific decorator visionary on hand to transform the space into your wedding dream. With amazing beams overhead, great lighting, flowers, and a gorgeous color scheme, you win major points for what decorators call "the juxtaposition of styles."

76. *Ski Lodge:* Winter weddings held at ski lodges give you the excitement of a snowy vacation with all the skiing, snowboarding, and snowmobiling you could want, not to mention great bars and lounges with oversized fireplaces and hot spiked drinks, outdoor hot tubs, and incredible suites with great views of the mountains.

77. *Tropical Resort:* When you walk into a tropical resort, you just switch over into a different mindset, right? It's vacation, the sun is hot on your shoulders, a cool ocean air is whispering in the palm trees, a steel-drum band is playing, and you just relax. Add in the tropical flowers, food, and drinks and this wedding hot spot could be your special wedding dream come true.

Specialty Locations

78. Of course, there are some brides and grooms who want to go all-out original. Forget the traditional wedding; they're going someplace that might not *ever* have held a wedding before. For some, it might be one of those underwater weddings with bride and groom in scuba gear, or a sky-diving wedding. We've heard about everything from in-line skate weddings on a boardwalk to weddings in a wax museum. Playful couples who love their games might marry in an amusement park or at a Dave & Buster's (a national chain of bar/arcade establishments—very fun!). Couples can even marry at New York City's Grand Central Station, which has just recently opened its doors to weddings and grand affairs in a truly historical building. Unforgettable!

79.

Here are some individual elements to look for when selecting your location.

Views

• An ocean view
• A mountain view
• A view of the city lights
• A view of a golf course

Access to water

• Beach access
• Boats
• Marinas

Water features

• A waterfall
• Fountains
• Koi ponds
• Rushing river water

Greenery

• Spectacular gardens
• Flowering trees
• Trees that are changing color in autumn
• Open fields
• Forest clearings
• Grassy dunes on the beach
• Gazebos
• Trellises
• Garden benches
• Stone walls

- Cobblestone paths
- Wishing wells

In the building
- Outdoor terrace
- Poolside
- Elegant library
- Cigar bar
- Piano bar
- Floor-to-ceiling windows
- Balconies and alcoves
- Observatories

The Appeal of Great Lighting

The way a room or grounds are lit can make all the difference in the look and feel of any wedding location. I've pulled this out as a focal point to get you to consider different and enchanting ways any space can look with various lighting effects.

80. Imagine a regular ballroom with the main lights turned down and the room illuminated by the candles on each guest table, glowing amber-colored spotlights on the head table and the cake, and fun spotlighting on the dance floor. It makes the entire room look more elegant than if the house lights were on at full blast.

81. At an outdoor wedding, the tent would be lit inside by a system of spotlights and perhaps strings of little white lights (called "fairy lights") arranged at the ceiling of the tent, surrounding trees might also be lit with fairy lights, and nearby fountains can be lit up with blue or aqua-colored lights. We're going to get into *way* more detail on lighting décor for your wedding site in Chapters 17 and 18, but I wanted to get you looking at your potential wedding sites with an eye toward how you can transform a lovely location into something truly special with a few simple and creative lighting choices.

82. Remember, any site you look at, take a look at it at night. See how it's illuminated. Ask the site manager to show you what he or she can arrange for the lighting *at the time your wedding will take place.* It's not good enough to see the place on a Sunday morning. You'll need to assess any location by how it will look at the time of your wedding. Great lighting can make all the difference.

The Appeal of Hotels

83. For the "full package" of a different, more expansive variety, look to hotels and resorts not only for their grand ballrooms but for the many additional advantages you get as part of being one of their wedding couples. Remember, it's not just the wedding day itself that you're planning, but—especially if you have many guests coming in from out of town to share in your big day—the entire wedding weekend. Staking your ground at a hotel or resort can give you a convenient home base where you and your guests have a buffet of entertainment and activity options just an elevator ride away. The convenience of having the following on site can make a hotel ballroom automatically become a more attractive option for your reception.

• Spa and salon
• *Lounges*
• *Several restaurants on site*
• *Fitness center*
• *Pools and whirlpools*
• *Children's game room and activities*
• *Outdoor activities*
• *Cocktail parties*
• *Free shuttles to nearby attractions and shopping*
• *Suites and penthouses*
• *Room service*
• Internet-ready rooms

- *Freebies and discounts for you, like the honeymoon suite free with your booking of a certain number of rooms for your guests, free champagne in your suite, free massages at the spa, and any number of bride and groom perks*

A hotel setting for your wedding can provide many comforts for your guests and countless enjoyable activity options that *you* might otherwise have had to plan individually had you not chosen the hotel as your site.

PART TWO:

Planning Your Ceremony

chapter 5

Building a Beautiful Ceremony That's You

For any wedding, it's not just about the dress or the cake or the band. Those might seem like the most important things to plan, but the *real* centerpiece of your day is the ceremony. After all, exchanging vows and rings and sealing the covenant of marriage is the whole purpose of the day. The rest is just icing on the cake.

84. Get your priorities in line. So many couples get lost in the pretty details of the flowers, the champagne, the limousines, and the designer dresses that they initially gloss over the really important stuff. Getting married isn't about having a big party where you're the center of attention. That's exactly where so many couples make a big mistake. It's about the enormity of your decision to join your lives together forever, to make big promises, and to become to each other something new and everlasting. If you're a person of deep faith, the ceremony has a very sacred meaning to you, in addition to the sentimental meaning.

So, knowing that the ceremony is not just a formality to get to the big party and the big gifts, here is where you'll start forming your designs for the perfect marriage rituals and words.

Whose House?

85. If you regularly attended church or synagogue throughout your life, and you belong to a particular house of worship, there might be no question that you'll marry at the place that feels like "home" to you.

86.
If you're far from the house of worship of your youth and not connected to any particular new church or synagogue, you might starting searching now for a new spiritual "home." Considering that some churches and synagogues will only marry members or parishioners—no exceptions—it might be a wise idea for you to start attending services where you are now. As an added bonus, many couples report that this task of searching for a new congregation actually brought a much-valued return to their beliefs, and an even greater bond with their partner.

87.
If marrying in a house of worship is more important to your significant other than to you, and he or she is of a different faith than yours, then by all means consider offering to marry in his or her choice of church or synagogue as a special compromise, and something that will be very important to your partner (and perhaps your partner's family).

88. If it's form over function that does it for you, you might look for architecturally gorgeous houses of worship where you can hold your wedding. For some couples who consider themselves to be more spiritual than religious, but still want to honor family beliefs and marry in a church, this could be the answer. Tour houses of worship with an eye toward how it looks and feels to you, as well as how the officiant acts with you, and this could be the right setting for your wedding.

89. Marry in a nonreligious setting. Whether it's the outdoors, your home, or a separately decorated area of your reception locale, all you need to do is set up an altar, trellis, or chuppah, line up chairs, form your aisle, decorate as you please, and create your own ceremony site. Countless couples have done this on the beach, in particular, or poolside or under a giant tree in their yard (this is extra sentimental if one or both partners used to climb that tree as a child). Sometimes creating your own ceremony site (and being free to make your own ceremony rules!) is just what it takes to make a wedding extra special.

Who's Doing the Ceremony?

90. For many couples, their wedding is extra special when the ceremony is performed by the priest, minister, rabbi, or officiant who has been a big part of their lives. Perhaps it's the priest who, in his younger days, was the one who christened you, the pastor who led you through the confirmation process, or the rabbi who taught your religious classes. If you have a particularly fond connection with any religious officiant, it might be worth any extra mile taken to have him or her be the one to perform your wedding ceremony. This level of sentimentality brings your life full circle in a sense, which could be a very special addition to your day.

91. One of the most popular trends right now follows the example of a certain *Friends* wedding episode, where Joey gets ordained as a minister to marry Monica and Chandler. Now thousands upon thousands of couples are writing in to ask how they can have a friend or relative become ordained and able to perform their wedding ceremonies. Some states like California have clearly set laws and rules that easily allow a regular citizen to get ordained for a day, while others will be more of a challenge. Rather than take any Internet "get ordained" site at its word as far as legal matters in each state, call your county courthouse to ask about your state's applicable rules about personal ordination and who your state recognizes as a legal minister for your wedding. The extra research could be worth it to you, as so many couples married by friends, fathers, and godparents say that having a loved one lead their rites was incredibly special in itself. Who better to do the job than someone who loves you?

92. Any ordained officiant can be found through wedding channels, searches, and word-of-mouth referrals from friends. Especially if you're a spiritual couple with quasi–New Age leanings, you'll find plenty of interesting and unique brands of officiants out there. From Native American ministers to Wiccan priestesses, spiritual leaders to certified interfaith ministers, you have your choice of the many flavors of officiants available to work your wedding your way.

93. The most common brand of interfaith or nondenominational minister-for-hire is ready, willing, and able to work *with* you to write and create a truly personalized wedding ceremony complete with any favorite readings, poetry, cultural rituals, and music you have in mind. Interview well, meet with potential candidates, look through their sample books of previous ceremonies, and find the one that most matches your desired style of ceremony.

Finding Your Style

94. For you, the word "special" might mean having an ultra-traditional ceremony, with every word handed down to you by the canons of your religion. Every portion of the ceremony comes right from the script, from the way your parents and grandparents conducted their wedding rituals, and you wouldn't have it any other way.

Are You Traditional?

According to a survey by *WeddingBells* magazine, 88 percent of brides and grooms say that their wedding ceremonies will be "traditional."

95. Mix up ultra-traditional with a few modern touches. Many couples are taking the ancient wedding script and splashing it with a little bit of sanctioned personalization. That could be a special rose ceremony where you present white roses to your mothers as a thank you for their years of guidance, or the presentation by both of you of a separate candle lit in memory of departed loved ones. Today's houses of worship, even the most strict, might surprise you with their willingness to let you get creative with their wedding scripts. So see which symbolic moves you might want to make, and ask your officiant for the okay before you arrange anything.

96. You may choose to forget the scripts of tradition. Your ceremony held outside of a house of worship might just gloss over the religious aspect of the marriage rites and take another path. Couples who call themselves individualists are very happy to make their weddings special by writing their ceremonies from scratch. Every reading, every vow, every musical selection and symbolic rite comes right from *their* wishes and not from any prescribed list; more on this in the next chapter. For now, see if you two would like to throw tradition to the wind when it comes to your ceremony and create a new look and feel for your own.

chapter 6

Wedding Vows

It's not enough for a ceremony to be beautiful on the outside, with perfect décor in a lovely setting, and the two of you looking your all-time best. What truly makes any wedding ceremony special is the meaning within it. That means the words you speak, the music performed, the sentimental and symbolic gestures you make, and the people who are there to share and participate in it. The words for your wedding are what make this centerpiece portion of your day truly the most beautiful of all.

In this section, you'll begin to craft your ceremony from a veritable blank slate, filling it with meaning and the words of your heart. You'll make it your own; a reflection of who the two of you are and what you find most important in each other, in your partnership, in marriage, and in love universally. Let's get started going through the sections of your ceremony and how you can make them extra special to you and to everyone in attendance.

The Arrival

Before even a word is spoken, it's all about the opening impression, making a beautiful arrival and setting the stage and the mood for the ceremony at hand. Here are some tips to make the first moments of your wedding extra special.

As Guests Arrive

97. Impress them at the start and transport them to your wedding vision with beautiful décor, such as fabric drapings, floral arrangements, and lit candles.

98. The music that is playing as guests arrive is a terrific mood setter. Consider classical music such as Rachmaninov's *Rhapsody on a Theme of Paganini*, or Vivaldi's *The Four Seasons*. You can also hire a harpist, cellist, or flutist to play live classical music as your wedding soundtrack.

99. Instruct your groomsmen or ushers to make friendly small talk with guests as they are seating them. This warm and personable welcome goes a long way toward putting guests at ease and inviting them into a comfortable frame of mind.

100. Have ushers and groomsmen present each female guest with a single long-stemmed rose or small bunch of flowers tied with a ribbon and a preprinted welcome note from you. This very special opening gesture reminds the guests that even now, during your big moment on your big day, you are happy that they have come to be with you.

101. Station "hosts" at the ceremony entrance door. Choose one from each side of your families who is likely to recognize guests and provide a familiar face as guests arrive. This starts the event off with a note of ease, and allows someone "in the know" to instruct ushers on where to seat the most special guests, and better facilitate guests to be seated with the people they know.

For the Parents

102. Have special music playing as the mother of the bride, mother of the groom, and father of the groom are being escorted down the aisle and led to their seats. Choose a song that is special to them.

103. Arrange to have single roses placed at the mothers' seats before they are escorted to their places.

104. Arrange to have a card or note of thanks from you, or from both you and the groom, waiting for them at their seats as well.

105. Arrange to have a small, wrapped gift waiting for the parents at their seats, as a token of your appreciation for all of their help with the wedding. Some ideas might be a bracelet or heart-shaped locket for the mothers ("Mom, you'll always be a part of my heart"), or even tickets to a big special event that you will attend with your parents after the honeymoon (as in, "Don't worry…we're still going to spend a lot of time with you even after we're married").

For the Groom

106. As the groom awaits the start of the ceremony, tucked back in a secluded room, perhaps nervously rehearsing his vows and wiping beads of sweat from his forehead, this would be the perfect time to have a card, note, or gift delivered to him from the bride. A simple "I can't wait to marry you!" or "I'm so happy you're mine" will be an unforgettable moment for him.

107. This might also be a great time for your father to step back into the groom's holding cell to shake his hand and welcome him to the family.

108. If the best man is waiting with the groom, this could also be a great time for him to say a few words of encouragement, give him a gift, or crack a joke to put the groom at ease.

109. When the officiant calls and it's time for the groom to step out into the spotlight, he might want to enter to the notes of a song that he has chosen as *his* entry music. Why not? The bride usually has free reign to choose the music she'd like to make her entrance to. Why not the groom as well? It could be an expertly edited portion of classical music that's appropriate for a formal wedding, live trumpeters sounding a regal call to announce the big moment, or—at a less formal wedding where laughs are appropriate—it could be his "theme song." For example, he can use the music from the Robert Redford baseball movie *The Natural.* This song gave the guests a giggle at one real wedding when the groom stepped out of the vestibule, slowly pointed to where the bride was about to enter, and then took his place at the altar. (If you know the scene from the movie, you know what I'm talking about!)

110. Just as the mothers of the bride and groom are being seated—traditionally the last to be seated before the bride's entrance—the groom might take a moment to present each mother (plus additional stepmothers, if applicable) with a single rose, a kiss on the cheek, a hug, and words of gratitude. You can't start the mothers off in a more special way than that.

For the Bridal Party

111. When the men take their places next to the groom, they can each shake his hand or hug him in congratulations. This is appropriate even at the most formal of wedding ceremonies, which in times past could seem almost too stuffy and stiff without this visual display of affection among the men. The guys are not lining up to await some morose event like a funeral, where the clasped hands and serious faces would be more appropriate. This is a celebration, so they can come out to handshakes and even fun high-fives if that is their group's style.

112. As the bridesmaids and maid of honor start making their way down the aisle, play a song that's perfect for their big entrance. It could be formal classical music. It could be, at a less formal wedding, something fun and playful that speaks of your relationship to the women themselves. Make it even better and surprise them with the song—don't have it played at the rehearsal.

113. Take the ritual of scattering rose petals out of the hands of just the flower girl and let all of the bridesmaids sprinkle the aisle with rose petals, to make it even more of a fragrant carpet for the good fortune of the bride to follow.

114. If everyone is scattering petals, then have the maid of honor sprinkle white rose petals as she walks, as a lovely bridal contrast to the red and pink ones the other maids have tossed.

For the Bride

115. Switch from the relaxing classical music that has been playing to a more dramatic, "announcement" type of music, such as the soaring strains of the "Bridal March," a more modern CD recording of the song you'll enter to, trumpet calls in true royal fashion, or the well-timed peal of the church bells marking the big moment.

116. Make it a big production. Have the church or ceremony location dim the house lights and turn on preplaced glowing lights aimed at the aisle where you will walk. Illuminate the altar where the groom is standing for the Hollywood treatment, a shift in ambience that says, "the show is about to begin." Your entrance is special and should be set apart from all others in a dramatic and elegant way. Lighting could be just the effect you'll love.

117. Tradition usually had the bride being escorted by her father down the aisle to her groom. Now, more and more brides are giving the honor to their father *and* mother.

118. Still others are having a stepfather take them halfway down the aisle, and a birth father take them the rest of the way.

119. Others have the two fathers escort her on either side.

120. Some brides without an active father figure choose to be escorted by their mothers.

121. Some brides who have children have the kids walk with them.

122. Others have a brother do the honors.

123. Of course, there are the independent twenty-first-century brides who wish for no one to "give them away." They'll walk towards their future husbands on their own, thank you very much.

124. At the end of the aisle, you can stop to kiss your mother and future mother-in-law, the fathers, or your kids before you take your future husband's hand for the start of the ceremony.

The Ceremony Begins

125. Rather than launch right into the traditional wedding text, your officiant could start off with something a little bit more personal about the two of you. Something along the lines of, "When Jeff and Carrie first came to ask me to perform their wedding ceremony, I knew right away that it was not going to be just any wedding. Carrie had definite ideas about what she wanted to say, and even what she hoped Jeff would say, and all along Jeff just sat back and looked at Carrie with a complete look of adoration. None of us here today can have any question that these two are perfect for one another, and it is our honor to be a part of their special moment."

126. Before the officiant begins, he might make reference to any of the cultural or religious elements that are about to be part of the ceremony. "Jeff and Carrie have arranged for their wedding to include his German heritage as well as her Korean heritage. Throughout this ceremony, we will enact some of the most symbolic rituals from both of their backgrounds, as it is their wish to honor their ancestry and their roots, their families, and their values."

127. The officiant can also make mention that a complete description of each of the rituals' meanings can be found printed on the back page of the wedding program, where you've detailed the deep symbolic explanation of every ceremony element. Guests love being able to follow along with what's going on, they may learn something new about your culture, and having these explanations brings the special significance of each step to life for them.

Readings

128. In the ceremony, you might include special readings, such as the ever-popular wedding script of 1 Corinthians 13:

[1]If I speak in the tongues of men and of angels, but have not love, I am only a resounding gong or a clanging cymbal. [2]If I have the gift of prophecy and can fathom all

mysteries and all knowledge, and if I have a faith that can move mountains, but have not love, I am nothing. ³If I give all I possess to the poor and surrender my body to the flames, but have not love, I gain nothing. ⁴Love is patient, love is kind. It does not envy, it does not boast, it is not proud. ⁵It is not rude, it is not self-seeking, it is not easily angered, it keeps no record of wrongs. ⁶Love does not delight in evil but rejoices with the truth. ⁷It always protects, always trusts, always hopes, always perseveres. ⁸Love never fails. But where there are prophecies, they will cease; where there are tongues, they will be stilled; where there is knowledge, it will pass away. ⁹For we know in part and we prophesy in part, ¹⁰but when perfection comes, the imperfect disappears. ¹¹When I was a child, I talked like a child, I thought like a child, I reasoned like a child. When I became a man, I put childish ways behind me. ¹²Now we see but a poor reflection as in a mirror [also "as through a glass darkly" or "as through a glass dimly"]; then we shall see face to face. Now I know in part; then I shall know fully, even as I am fully known. ¹³And now these three remain: faith, hope, and love. But the greatest of these is love.

129. For a wide-ranging selection of popular wedding ceremony readings, poetry, and quotes, go to:

www.weddingchannel.com
www.bridalguide.com
www.modernbride.com
www.theknot.com

130. Of course, you can always write your own poetry or readings from scratch. If you're a gifted writer, you might be able to pen just the right words, expressing all that both of you wish to have as a part of your wedding ceremony. While these are not your vows, you can expand on your thoughts about love and marriage to one another in a significant part of your ceremony.

131. Bestow a great honor on a friend, parent, child, or the person who introduced the two of you to one another by having *that* person be the one who stands up to read your chosen passages.

132. You can also ask a very close friend or family member to select or write their own special message for the ceremony.

Music

133. Having beautiful and meaningful music as a part of your ceremony makes the event that much more special. Choose from the approved list of secular and nonsecular songs allowed in your house of worship (remember, some houses are very strict about what they will and will not allow to take place during weddings).

134. If you have complete freedom with your music at your site, select the perfect songs to play as an interlude during your ceremony, such as when rituals are being prepared:
• Classical music
• Religious hymns
• Instrumental music
• Ethnic and cultural music
• Modern romantic songs

135. An extra-special touch is to have a specially written song, perhaps inspired by the two of you, performed at your ceremony. It could be the groom playing his guitar and singing to the bride (as he did on your first date), the bride singing to the groom, or a friend giving the couple the gift of a song written just for you. Such a personal touch makes any ceremony that much more special.

136. Depending on the site, such as at a church, you might be able to use their own choir, chorale, or children's chorus.

137. Some houses of worship might have their own list of approved musicians, along with an on-site harp or piano used in their services. Check on the sound system, too. Some of the new buildings are wired with surround sound, believe it or not.

138. Go traditional with the church organ.

139. Have your guests be part of the music. Provide the printed words to any songs being performed, and have the officiant ask your guests to sing along. This works beautifully in less formal weddings, such as on the beach or at a hotel ballroom, and it's particularly moving when the music in question is a traditional ethnic song that your guests sing in beautiful harmony. Among the most breathtaking weddings I've attended were the ones where cultural songs were sung meaningfully by guests among the shared heritage, and also lovely faithful songs sung by guests who belonged to the same church group as the bride and groom. Just beautiful.

140. The music need not claim its own separate spot in the ceremony. Consider having lilting instrumental music playing in the background the entire time. Such a soundtrack is an original twist on the old model ceremonies, and it's making a big rise in the trends today.

141. An island or beach wedding might have steel-drum music playing in the background, or use such traditional music as instrumental Hawaiian songs as your ceremony soundtrack.

142. If your background is Asian, bring the sounds of your culture to your ceremony by having Asian string music playing.

143. Very popular now is the Native American sound of drum music as a steady heartbeat to the proceedings, or lilting flute music. Check out the many instrumental recordings of R. Carlos Nakai. See if you can have these or other Native American music CDs played at your ceremony for an authentic mood.

144. Consider hiring professional musicians or singers to perform at your ceremony. It's not just the reception that gets such treatment. Countless brides and grooms have hired soloists and bagpipers for their big day, and so can you—along with ethnic music professionals, such as through www.musicintheair.com (in the New York area) and other musical entertainment association sites in cities near you. Check out www.ises.com for references to music and entertainment companies you can hire for your wedding.

Symbolic Gestures and "Moments"

145. The unity candle is the most widely recognized symbolic moment in a wedding ceremony. During this popular ritual, the bride and groom use two separate candles to light one larger pillar candle as a symbol of their two "lights" coming together as one. In some unity candle rituals, the mothers are asked to come up and light the two individual candles as a symbol of the two individual families that the bride and groom were raised in.

146. Another twist on this ritual is the wine ceremony, also a sake ceremony in some Asian cultures, where the bride and groom take a sip from the same glass as a symbol of their shared celebration and nourishment.

147. In some cultures, the bride and groom are presented with a piece of bread to symbolize a good harvest, a sip of wine for prosperity, and a saucer of salt to keep the flavor in the marriage. (Different cultures define the bread, wine, and salt with their own meanings, so expect to find some variation on this as you do your research.)

148. The bride and groom might be crowned with olive leaves, floral wreaths, or actual gold crowns as they take their vows. Some say this symbolizes the couple as king and queen of their home, and true partners on a pedestal.

149. Bride and groom might also be bound together at the wrists (lightly, of course) with a rope cord, braided silk, a rosary, or a greenery and floral garland, symbolizing their joining together as husband and wife (i.e., no one can sever their connection). This ritual comes in many forms, sometimes referred to as "handfasting."

150. In some cultures, the bride's head is covered with a length of lace fabric, while the fabric is reached over to cover the groom's shoulder, also binding them together.

151. The bride and groom might be showered with any number of objects in the course of their ceremony. In some cultures it's figs, in others, it's almonds. In still others, it might be sweets. All symbolize their shared good fortune and health in their long life together.

152. In Asian cultures, there might be a traditional tea ceremony, where the bride and groom serve one another and their family members a cup of tea in an elaborately and finely tuned ritual.

153. During some ceremonies, the guests are encouraged to extend greetings and peace to their neighbors where they sit. If your house of worship enacts this traditional ritual, you might choose to walk down to where your family is sitting and extend your greetings and peace to them as well.

154. During the ceremony, you might wish to have a moment of silence or a song performed in memory of departed loved ones who couldn't be there for your day. In some families, roses are tossed into the ocean or a wreath is tossed from a boat into the water. A small bouquet of flowers or a single boutonniere might be placed on an empty chair to symbolize the "presence" of a departed loved one.

Your Wedding Program

155. Printed wedding programs let your guests know the name of that beautiful song you've chosen for your processional, the meanings of your rituals, and the names of all the major players in your family and bridal party. Use this program as a way to let guests know what's going on and even participate.

156. You can order professionally printed programs, or make them yourselves on your home computer using a great graphics and layout program, lovely paper, and a graphic cover.

157. Consider printing a special message of thanks from the two of you to your parents, in-laws, and your guests for helping with and attending the wedding.

158. Lay out a boxed poem or quote that's important to you.

159. Include a digital image of the two of you to further personalize your program.

160. Provide your new home address and contact information on the back of the program so that all of your loved ones can stay in touch with you in the future.

161. A great touch provided in the wedding programs: a single facial tissue in white or your wedding color scheme. Your guests will certainly be brought to tears by the beauty and sentiments of your ceremony!

Your Vows

162. For you, reciting the traditional wedding vows your parents took at their wedding (e.g., "to love, honor, and cherish…to have and to hold from this day forward, forsaking all others…") might be the perfect way to add special meaning to your ceremony. Ask your officiant to hand you the traditional script and follow it to the letter.

163. Another option is to make a few stylistic changes to the wording, as allowed by the house of worship. For instance, you might want to scratch out "obey" and add "support and respect."

164. Writing your own vows is the perfect way to make your ceremony more meaningful, as the words come from your own heart and the individual building blocks of your relationship. If this appeals to you, spend plenty of time thinking about and writing your own vows.

165. You can write one set of personalized vows that you'll both speak to one another.

166. You can surprise one another with the vows you've written to each other.

167. For much more on the ins and outs of writing your own wedding vows, pick up a copy of *Your Special Wedding Vows*, available at your local bookstore or by calling Sourcebooks at 800-727-8866.

168. Include your own favorite classic poetry or quotes—the words written by literary greats, world leaders, and philosophers who have mastered the art of writing about love and eternity.

169. Mix up "borrowed" quotes with your own expansion on the theme, such as with "Grow old along with me, the best is yet to be" by Robert Browning. Take his original and timeless romantic saying, and expound on it with something along the lines of "And I know that as we grow old together, we'll grow even more beautiful and valuable to one another, our bond strengthened over time. Let us look forward to all the best that is yet to be, together, hand-in-hand, for all time."

170. Use a letter as part of your vows, perhaps reading from your diary entry on the day you met, reading from a love letter you wrote to your intended, or that he wrote to you. Share these private words only with full permission from your partner, though. Some things have been written for your eyes only!

171. If you have many guests who have come from overseas and speak little English, repeat your vows in the language of your heritage, for full inclusion of all.

172. If you have one or more guests who are deaf or hearing impaired, hire a sign language expert to illustrate the events of your ceremony. Similarly, in the case of one wedding where the bride's mother was legally blind, the couple hired a speaking commentator to describe in vivid, beautiful detail everything that was taking place during the ceremony. The bride's mother was so grateful not to miss a moment.

The Exchange of Rings

173. If you have had a special sentiment engraved on the inside of your rings, such as "forever yours," "my heart," or something equally precious, have the officiant share that with all of your guests. "Seth and Kelly have chosen to inscribe the word 'forever' on the inside of their wedding bands, and as they exchange their wedding rings now, they make a promise to love and support one another forever."

174. For the groom: kiss the ring, and then kiss the hand that will wear it before slipping it onto her finger.

175. Both bride and groom might choose to kiss the rings before presenting them to one another.

176. If the marriage is between people who have children from prior relationships, or a child or children of their own, they can present rings to the children as well. Make them a birthstone or diamond chip for extra-special meaning.

chapter 7

Closing Your Ceremony

Once the vows are spoken, the rings exchanged, and the marriage sealed with a kiss, the applause sounds and you're on your way! Here are some tips to make your departure a stylish and spectacular one.

177. Take a bow! Pause before your trip back down the aisle and soak up the group joy.

178. Stop before you walk any farther and hug your parents.

179. If you're holding an African American inspired wedding, jump the broom.

180. Run back down the aisle together and get a few extra seconds of kissing time before your bridal party and guests mob you outside the ceremony area.

181. Have the church bells ringing as you make your exit, a grand celebration the whole town will hear.

182. Pop a breath mint before you greet guests. Nervousness can cause dry mouth.

183. If your site allows, pop the corks on some champagne and have a toast out by the limousine.

184. Have live doves or butterflies released as you make your departure.

185. Complying with state and town laws, for an evening wedding, have fireworks timed to go off as you step outside.

186. Time your wedding to end as nearby town fireworks—such as on the Fourth of July—are just getting underway in the distance. All the spectacular effect with none of the cost or legal paperwork!

187. Have guests shower you with birdseed or flower petals—after getting permission, of course—or have them ring mini bells or blow bubbles as you zip by.

188. Have music playing for your big getaway. Choose a celebratory song, one that gets the party underway.

The Receiving Line

189. Whether you'll have your receiving line right outside the ceremony site, or set up at the reception area, include the entire bridal party and the parents as well.

190. Add on to the traditional receiving line. Grandparents, godparents, and the couple's children can stand in the line as well.

191. Include the couple who introduced the two of you. What an honor for them! This day wouldn't be happening without them.

192. Have waiters bring glasses of champagne or ice water with lemon to the members of the receiving line.

193. As a helpful note, have the last person in the receiving line hand out printed directions to the reception site. Some guests might have forgotten their printed directions from their invitation, and some guests might not be familiar with the area. It's a great courtesy for your guests who are driving.

Some Time Alone

194. If time permits, schedule into your day a solid hour between your ceremony and reception. This gives you a little bit of downtime and a chance for the big step you've just taken to sink in, and it also gives you private time with your bridal party and close family before the activities of the evening begin.

195. Scheduling a delay before your reception starts also gives you a chance to pose unhurriedly for pictures. There will be no stress, no rushing the photographer, no worrying about how much of your cocktail hour you're missing.

196. A break gives guests a chance to return to their homes or hotels to change for the reception or to stop in and check on their kids.

197. Arrange for a pre-cocktail hour at the reception site. You might be able to work it out with the site manager to have your guests led to the restaurant or hotel's bar or sports bar where they can mix, mingle, have a drink, and relax a bit before the reception begins.

198. At this pre-cocktail hour, guests can be given decorative vouchers good for a free drink at the hotel bar. Talk to the hotel manager about this. Some hotels already have free drink vouchers created for their overnight guests. This way, you very graciously prevent your guests from having to shell out any extra cash for their drinks. That's good forethought.

199. Use your time alone wisely. You might decide to spend it with your family and bridal party, in a smaller, more intimate setting for your first champagne toast.

200. You could also go off alone, just the two of you, for a walk through the gardens, a ride in the limo, or private time in the bridal suite at the reception hall. During this time, you can share your feelings, talk about your version of what happened before the wedding, how you felt when you first saw each other…those great in-the-moment reflections you won't have much privacy to share for the next few hours.

201. During your alone time, propose toasts to one another, for your ears only.

202. Give each other special gifts, your first exchange as husband and wife.

Part Three

Dressing Up in Style

chapter 8

Gorgeous Gowns and Colors for You

Your wedding gown may be the one thing you've always dreamt about. Perhaps you've imagined yourself in a long, flowing traditional gown. Or a sexier strapless gown with a beaded bodice. Maybe by now you've already twirled in front of a mirror as you tried on a few potential dresses. Whatever stage you're at—dreaming or searching—keep in mind that your goal is to find the perfect gown that's the most *you,* that one special find out of thousands. You'll know it the moment it is zipped up around you, since this one will just *feel* right. You'll feel like a bride in it.

In this section, you'll discover many options to make your wedding gown something spectacular. *(Note: the tips with stars next to them also apply to your bridesmaids' gowns.)*

The Dress

According to *WeddingBells* magazine's most recent survey, 85 percent of engaged women are planning to wear a dress that is long, traditional, and either white or ivory.

203. With only 85 percent of brides going the traditional route of the formal white wedding gown, that shows the door is being kicked wide open by brides in their strappy white heels, looking for new style alternatives for their gowns. You, too, might choose to search for something a little bit "outside the box," more stylish and sophisticated, or sexier.

*204. The trend in wedding gowns is now moving outside the traditional lines and laces and formal princess styles to borrow design elements from high fashion. What you'll see on the runways at bridal fashion shows and in bridal magazine photo spreads looks more like a great line of stylish party and event dresses than the traditional wedding gowns of yesteryear. So consider your favorite necklines, cuts, and dress shapes in fashion in general and slide that right into your wedding gown search.

205. Wedding gowns are showing lots of skin. From strapless to backless to bare arms and even dramatic, sexy slits, it's all about showing off that great body you've been working so hard to shape up. No more covering up from head to toe, encasing your arms in alençon lace—skin is the new accessory of choice for wedding gowns.

206. Remember that's it's your *face* you want to show off first. So one of the first decisions you should make is which neckline will flatter you most. A sweetheart neckline is flattering on most brides, but you might find that your face is most flattered by a square or scoop neckline, or even a high neck or halter-top. This is one of the first things gown designers and gown stylists ask brides who come in for dress shopping excursions. You might wish to wear dazzling jewelry too, a dramatic necklace perhaps, so be sure your gown's neckline will allow you room.

207. If you love the look of strapless but are just a little bit too blessed on top to pull it off, you can still attain that sexy strapless look with clear shoulder straps holding your bodice in place.

*208. Try one of the newest sophisticated styles: the halter top. Especially if it bares half or all of your back, this style that ties or attaches at the back of your neck is the look of the moment; perfect for formal through informal wedding styles.

209. Go for color! One of the best new ways to make your wedding dress extra-special is to incorporate color where once there was traditional, virginal all-white or cream-colored fabric. You can go for a blush pink gown, blush lilac, or a blush baby blue.

210. The new wow factor in wedding gowns is metallic: silver, gold, and copper.

211. First-time brides especially are going for color in their gowns, regardless of what tradition has to say. If choosing a colored gown goes a bit too far in the "bucking tradition" department, you can do as many others have done and just have some color accenting your white or ivory gown. For example, include a sprinkling of blush pink crystals in the bodice of your gown amongst the clear beads.

212. Try using a blush-colored pearl for every white pearl in your accented bodice, skirt, or train.

*213. Go floral with blush pastels or even bold reds in designs sewn into your gown's bodice, skirt, train, or veil.

*214. Choose shimmer over color with light-reflecting beading in your gown's accents.

*215. Go for eye-catching shimmer in the all-white, cream, or blush fabric of your gown. Some of the newest, hottest fabrics out there are designed to catch the light and sparkle.

*216. Use ribbons in your gown. They can be artfully woven into the hem of your gown, tied in romantic bows at the base of your back, or used to accent your waistline or neckline.

217. Use fabric flowers in the design of your gown. Whether they're of the same white silk as your gown, or a blush pink, sage green, lilac, blue, or butter yellow, hand-designed fabric roses can be bunched at the base of your back (especially great if you have a plunging backline) or at the hem of your gown.

*218. Use gathering. Imagine this: portions of your gown's skirt are held up like a theater curtain as it rises, attached with a pearl or crystal accent. This draped effect is hot on the runways, and adds a bit of drama to a skirt when the bodice is simple.

219. Use "illusion" netting to demurely cover a plunging neckline, to cover your shoulders and the tops of your arms, or to add some see-through drama to a plunging backline.

*220. Use an overlay. A simple sheath gown that hangs straight down, unadorned, can be dressed up with a length of chiffon or layered lace to add a special element to an elegant gown.

221. The layering phenomenon is growing in the wedding gown world. Now, you can wear a beautifully designed full-length lace "jacket" that covers your arms and reaches to the floor during your ceremony, and then remove the lace jacket to reveal a simple, sexy, elegant, evening-wear gown for your reception. This is a stylish solution for situations where your house of worship does not allow bare shoulders.

222. Lace is coming back in full force. Explore the many varieties of lace out there, from Italian to French to Asian. You'll find a multitude of designs for everything from jackets to sleeves to bodices; even entire trains made out of beautiful lace. Look for Chantilly, alençon, and the intricate antique designs that artisans of yesteryear have created by hand.

223. Lace is also feeding into that bare-skin trend. Look for gowns that use lace as the *skirt* at thigh-height.

*224. Go retro. 1920s and 1930s flapper styles are all the rage, due to the popularity of the movie and musical *Chicago*. No, this isn't a passing fancy; flapper-inspired designs have stood the test of time. So look to see if beautifully draping beadwork and thin silk fringe, gathered bodices, and lots of leg will make a plain gown something special.

*225. Take a simple sheath gown and make it something movie-star special by draping a scarf around your neck and letting it hang loosely down your back—very Grace Kelly.

*226. Look at dress sculpture. Designers are taking lengths of lace and twisting them to make surprisingly pretty shoulder straps with keyhole necklines.

227. Copy a celebrity bride's style. Loved Jennifer Aniston's classic wedding dress? Take a photo to a designer or professional seamstress who can make you a copy altered to suit your body shape and best features.

*228. Play with pleating. Side pleats make a big impact when chosen instead of a back pleat.

*229. Play with shirring. This gathered, almost pinched line of your bodice and gown front is flattering to some body shapes, and it's a highly styled accent for a gown.

230. Play with trains. From a long, cathedral-length train suitable for an ultra-formal gown to the sweep of a chapel-length train, think about the style, formality, and location of your wedding when you look at fabric designs and styles for your train.

231. Don't have a train at all! Some brides don't want to be bothered with needing two bridesmaids to pick up and move her skirt when she needs to turn at the ceremony, and the whole idea of pinning up ten pounds of fabric into a bustle to lug around all night is just a headache. You can be formal and bridal without one.

232. Use shape in your fabric. The biggest designers out there are using fabrics that are dotted and even imprinted with little fabric hearts or stars. Look at alternative fabrics for a one-of-a-kind special gown look.

*233. Go light and airy with silk chiffon and silk crepe. Especially for warm-weather months or destination weddings, it's this lighter-than-air look that can make your perfect bridal gown come to life.

*234. Go short! Fun bridal styles are coming out in mid-calf and shorter styles for fun, less formal weddings, beach weddings, and cocktail-style reception weddings. Plus, this style shows off your fabulous shoes!

*235. Choose a convertible gown. By this, I mean your gown has a little magic to it with a train that can be removed, sleeves that can be removed, even a long, traditional skirt that comes off to reveal a sexier, slitted skirt for the evening's party.

236. Forget the transformer gown and buy two separate ones! Especially since you can now find great gowns at low prices out there, do as celebrity brides and socialites do and have one gown for the ceremony and then a sexier party dress for the reception—and maybe even a third outfit for your departure at the end of the night. Why not wow your crowd more than once?!

Finding the Gown

237. You might be surprised to know that only about 2 percent of brides shop for their gowns in big, flashy bridal boutiques without checking anywhere else. There are great deals to be had in a number of places, so spread out your search.

*238. Check the smaller dress shops for their bridal gown offerings. I found my $3,000 Scott McClintock bridal gown for just $300 at a little hole-in-the-wall dress shop in a town right by me—and right around the corner from a big bridal gown boutique.

239. Shop sample sales and designer trunk sales to find marked-down styles that might be perfect for you.

240. Check out department stores. Often these have bridal gowns in stock, along with stylish white, off-white, or blush-color formal gowns that would make perfect bridal gowns in the style of your choice. Hit these stores right before the holidays, and also at sale time, to get a great selection at a welcome price.

241. Take a chance and stop in at consignment shops. Countless brides unload gowns they won't use or don't want to keep (as in the case of a cancelled wedding, divorce, or just buying the wrong gown on sale) at a consignment store. That's where my $3,000 Scott McClintock gown wound up, probably going to some lucky bride for $100 or less! You never know!

242. Take your chances on eBay or some online auction site where you'll find a ton of designer wedding gowns at auction. Just be careful and realize that you shop at your own risk when using online auction sites. Be smart, follow good e-consumer rules, and protect your investment.

243. Not the sentimental type? Don't dream about boxing up your wedding gown to pass down to your daughter or making a christening dress out of it for your future baby? See no need to preserve your gown for decades to come? If keeping your gown is not on your list of wishes, and you can't fathom spending thousands of dollars for a gown you'll wear once in your life, then you might wish to consider renting your wedding gown. It's actually far from cheesy, and gown rental agencies are rounding up great designer styles from sample sales and trunk sales to rent them out only three to four times each. Check out the options and see if this special rental is the way to go.

244. Use an heirloom gown. If your mom had her wedding gown well-preserved and you love the style and sentimentality of getting married in your mother's (or mother-in-law's or grandmother's) gown, then take it in for alterations and you have a priceless, special gown for a very, very low expense.

245. Have your mother's gown style copied by a professional dress designer or wedding-specialist seamstress. The sentiment is the same, even if the fabric is new.

246. Similarly, you can take a portion of an heirloom gown, such as a lace train, and have it added to your new simple and stylish gown. Now that's a memory for both of you, and you won't spend thousands for a new designer one.

247. If part of your ceremony will have an ethnic or multicultural emphasis, you might wish to use special ceremonial robes or a ceremonial gown in the first part of your modern ceremony. Shop for beautiful ceremonial gowns in red or gold, as defined by your heritage, or borrow a relative's or friend's gown, provided you strike an agreement with her about any alterations or payment for damages first.

Holding Onto Your Gown After the Wedding

248. Like the majority of brides, you can have your gown professionally cleaned and sealed for eternal preservation in an air-tight case, and hold on to it to give to your daughter someday. (Be sure to have this done within six months of your wedding to prevent irreversible damage to the gown from stains that have set.)

249. You can do as many brides are doing and have the dress itself redesigned and altered to make it a gown that can be worn many more times; such as a stylish little black dress you'll wear for years to come.

chapter 9

Gorgeous Gowns and Colors for Your Bridesmaids

As mentioned at the start of Chapter 8, the starred tips also apply to your bridesmaids' gowns. After all, both you and they have access to stylish and sophisticated designer styles in wedding day dresses, great colors, and sexy accents that are right off the runway. This is a great time in fashion for bridesmaids and maids of honor, so here are some additional tips for their perfect, and perhaps personalized, wedding day look.

250. By far, the best way to make your bridesmaids' gowns special is to pick the color, and then have *them* choose the style of dress that works best and is most flattering to them. For instance, one might want to go strapless, and another might love to wear a halter. If the color is exact, and of course the skirt lengths uniform, give your bridesmaids the freedom to choose their own tops.

Choosing a Top

251. This is just a partial list of the kinds of tops that can be mixed and matched among your bridesmaids. Consider the following:

- Strapless
- Halter
- Sleeveless
- Sheer sleeve
- Drape neck
- High neck
- Square neck
- Princess
- Corset
- Asymmetrical
- Jacketed
- Three-quarter-length sleeve
- Keyhole neckline
- Embroidery at neckline
- Embroidery on sleeves
- Plunging backline
- More cleavage/less cleavage

252. Skirts can also be mixed and matched. With the length of skirt announced by you, your bridesmaids will be free to choose from the following:

• Sheath or slim skirt
• Slitted slim skirt
• A-line skirt
• Flared-back skirt
• Skirt with pleating or draping
• Skirt with or without beaded accents

253. Dress up a plain skirt with an overlay, such as chiffon or organza, for a flowy, ballet-type look.

254. Set your maid of honor apart from the other attendants by choosing a different top style from the other bridesmaids (if the rest will be a uniform style). Perhaps she can be the one in the halter top, for instance.

255. Another way to set your maid of honor apart: choose a dress for her that's in a slightly different and color-coordinated hue from the others. For instance, she might be in a hunter green, while all the rest are in sage green.

256. Go for great color for all of your bridesmaids. Consider their coloring and the tones they'd feel most comfortable wearing, and then check out the many color options open to your group.

257. Look at the new metallics, especially the golds, silvers, and coppers. These tones flatter most complexions, and they're very hot for right now.

258. Go for bright candy colors, a stylish look that gets you away from ho-hum pastels.

259. Choose a color your bridesmaids are most likely to wear again in the future. Bridesmaids tell me that they get very excited about being allowed to choose a black or red dress, but butter yellow and orange don't thrill them, even if they work with your wedding color scheme. Ask them for hints about which colors they would definitely prefer to wear again.

260. Choose a color that works with the season of your wedding. If you're having an autumn wedding, go for rich golds and burgundies, hunter greens, and metallic coppers—the colors of the changing leaves. In winter, red has holiday cheer written all over it.

261. Look away from solids—geometrical prints and florals are following in high fashion's footsteps, opening the door for print bridesmaids' dresses. Chosen well, this can be a knockout look.

262. Pregnant bridesmaids will find great designer maternity dresses and gowns on the market in gorgeous styles that flatter, some with adjustable tie straps in back for an assured fit. Another option is to check out empire-waist gowns that allow for plenty of room. Thank all those celebrity moms-to-be out there for making maternity formalwear something that today's designers have really embraced. Now the pregnant bridesmaid gets to be radiant in a custom and comfortable gown, not squeezed into a matching set with the other bridesmaids.

Shoes and Accessories for Bridesmaids

263. Contrary to popular belief, your bridesmaids do *not* have to all buy the same style of shoe. Especially if they'll wear long dresses, it's fine to let them choose their own style of shoe in your prescribed heel height and open/closed toe selection.

264. If you're having the bridesmaids' shoes dyed to match, submit all the shoes in one order to the same store. Since different dyeing plants use slightly different mixtures of color, you could wind up with clashing colors if the bridesmaids have their shoes done at separate locations. Go through the trouble of ordering or collecting all the shoes, and have them all done together.

265. Your bridesmaids' jewelry, worn on the day of the wedding, can be extra-special if you make it your gift to them. Choose from diamond or pearl pendants, colored stone pendants, silver earrings, or jewelry sets as your thank you, and also as a keen way to get them to wear a uniform look in jewelry on the big day.

266. Allow the bridesmaids to wear their hair however they'd like. You're not a drill team. Not everyone has to have a French twist. This is where you allow their individuality and personal style to shine.

267. If they're looking for ideas in hair adornment, let them know that craft stores have very inexpensive pearl hair pins to be tucked into elaborate twists and braids.

268. Let your bridesmaids know about those teenage accessory shops in the mall, where simple colored or jeweled hairpins are plentiful and at lower costs than fine jewelry shops.

269. If your wedding will be outside or in colder weather, arrange to have your bridesmaids purchase matching wraps or jackets that go with their gowns.

270. Dress up your bridesmaids' look in that elegant Grace Kelly manner by having them drape scarves across their necks to hang loosely down their backs.

271. A beautiful shawl can be the answer to your house of worship's rules about "no bare shoulders." Have your bridesmaids choose from lovely lace shawls in great colors, finely crocheted silk shawls, or another wrap that works for during the ceremony.

272. Remember, panty hose shades need to match, especially if the bridesmaids will be wearing shorter skirts or skirts with slits. Make it a rule: suntan sandalfoot only. And get two pairs each in case of snags and runs.

273. Purchase small, circular or flower-shaped nonslip shoe pads for the insides of bridesmaids' shoes, especially if they'll be wearing high heels. These great little stickers sit inside the shoe and keep the bridesmaids' feet from sliding around or shifting in them. Check at shoe stores and department stores for these little pads, and stock up.

chapter 10

Wraps and Accessories for You

274. You, too, should purchase a wrap or shawl that coordinates with your gown if your wedding will be held in the cooler months. It's a much better look than draping your groom's tuxedo jacket around your shoulders.

275. In winter months, consider a faux fur muff for your hands, or a faux fur trim around your jacket. You can find old-fashioned Currier and Ives'–style designs, or high-fashion accessories with fur-type trim.

276. A bridal umbrella or parasol would be great for both rainy and sunny days. You can find these in craft shops or even party supply stores if you don't want to pay top dollar at bridal salons and department stores for a beautiful, unadorned, simple style of white or ivory umbrella.

277. For hot days, an Asian paper fan will come in handy. Choose a color, style, and design that works for you.

Shoes

278. Always go for wider, chunkier-heeled shoes if any part of your wedding will take place outdoors. These thicker heels will keep you from sinking into damp grass or having trouble on cobblestone paths and marble stairs.

279. If you're looking at jeweled strappy shoes, wear them for a while to be sure the jewel straps don't cut into your feet, ankles, or toes. Remember, you're going to be in these shoes for a long time on the wedding day.

280. Go for comfort. Choose simple-style shoes that are a great fit and feel natural on your feet.

281. Wear one pair of stylish heels for the ceremony, and then have a second pair of more comfortable shoes on hand to slip into for the reception. Some brides grab a pair of decorated sneakers or skimmers, and at the end of the night, they're thankful they went for the comfort fit.

282. Choose a lower-height heel, even if you know you look great in stilettos. You never know where your photographer might ask you to go to get those great photographs.

Jewelry

283. Wear the jewelry your groom gives you as his wedding gift to you. Many grooms offer their brides diamond pendants and earrings for just this reason.

284. Wear your mother's wedding day jewelry as a tribute to her.

285. Wear your own cherished cross or Star of David necklace on your wedding day.

286. Wear a family heirloom item of jewelry, such as the bracelet your grandmother wore at her wedding, on your wedding day.

287. Or wear an item of jewelry from the groom's side of the family, such as the bracelet his mother wore on her wedding day. Such an honor goes a long way in establishing a relationship with your new in-laws.

Your Veil

288. Beyond choosing a veil that looks beautiful with your gown and fits with the formality of your ceremony and wedding as a whole, it's a great idea to add a little extra something special to the veil or headpiece you've selected. From a design standpoint, look at intermittent crystal beading sewn in a well-spaced design all over the veil. This accent catches the light and makes your veil (and your glowing face behind it) just sparkle.

289. Add delicate lace accents to the body and hem of the veil.

290. Consider adding a gentle touch of color to your veil if you have color accents to your gown. A blush pink, shiny hem would work wonders.

291. Choose a transformer veil, one that starts off long at the reception, but then comes apart to reveal a smaller, more manageable style for the reception.

292. Remove the veil altogether at the reception, restyling your hair and perhaps inserting pearl pins or a jeweled hair comb for an entirely new look, ready for the party.

Dressing Your Head

293. Choose a tiara or headpiece that completes your bridal look and makes you feel like a princess. Try on a variety of styles and heights, always as you're wearing your gown, for the complete look.

Take that Tiara to Go

294. At www.wintersandrain.com, the tiara you purchase can be sent back to the company after the wedding to be restrung into a length of pearls, a pendant, earrings, a bracelet, or some other precious keepsake that you can wear again and again at special occasions.

295. Look at tiaras made not just of crystals and pearls (or the good stuff, diamonds and gemstones if you can afford it), but actual ceramic moldings of tiny, delicate flowers and leaves. Delicate as it may be, this design makes for a lovely headpiece.

296. Choose jeweled combs for a simpler look to pull back hair.

297. Style hair in an elegant chignon or molded style that needs no accent.

298. For informal or beach weddings, just wear your hair loose and curly with a single flower tucked behind your ear. You can't beat the all-natural, girl-next-door look.

299. Fasten tiny clip crystals into lengths of your hair to give your shiny mane some extra sparkle.

300. Use your Mom's headpiece (or your mother-in-law's or grandmother's) for a dose of family legacy and a touching tribute to the matriarchs of your family.

Something Old

You've heard the old adage "something old, something new, something borrowed, something blue," right? This traditional good luck ritual for any bride brings with it new, modern ways to pull it off.

301. Wear a family heirloom piece of jewelry.

302. Carry a sentimental handkerchief, such as one your mother or grandmother carried on her wedding day.

303. Get a new handkerchief monogrammed with your initials, and save it to hand down to your daughter someday.

304. Have a protective saint's medallion sewn into the underside hem of your skirt.

305. Attach the medallion to the handle of your bouquet.

306. If you can clean it well enough, wear your mother's, grandmother's, or mother-in-law's veil from her wedding day.

307. The same goes for any headpiece or tiara worn by a family member or friend, with a new veil attached.

Something New

308. Your wedding day jewelry, if given as a gift by your groom or your parents, would definitely count as a lucky something new.

309. It's not cheating to count your gown or your headpiece/veil as something new. You paid a fortune for it!

310. If your parents or in-laws give you a gift of jewelry in addition to that given by your groom, honor them by telling them that will be your "something new." Everyone likes to be in on this ritual, to make it complete for you.

Something Borrowed

311. If that headpiece or veil you're wearing is a temporary loan from a sister, friend, or parent, then that counts.

312. Your wedding day jewelry, such as the cross or diamond one of the moms lent you, can be your something borrowed.

313. The protective saint's medallion can also be borrowed.

Something Blue

314. A little blue trim on your garter works most often for today's brides.

315. Now that we're in the days of color for wedding gowns, perhaps you might choose a blush blue satin hemming or embroidery as your "something blue."

316. Your handkerchief can be a nice contrasting blue, or white with blue stitching.

317. Fun-loving brides, especially at beach weddings, have had their toenails painted a cloud blue.

318. If your birthstone is blue, then wear your birthstone earrings or a ring if they go with the colors of your hued gown.

319. One creative bride wrote in to tell me that her "something blue" was the color of her groom's eyes, which she loved.

Wedding Day Lingerie

320. Spend some money on the good stuff—high-end hosiery, garter belt, underwear, and a supportive bra that's the right style and cut for your gown.

321. Stock up on great lingerie for your wedding night and honeymoon.

322. Surprise your groom later that night. When he helps you remove your gown, have some fun underwear on, such as a thong with "I'm the Bride" printed in glitter across the front.

323. With all of those bridal showers coming up, you can hint to your maids that you have enough toasters and gadgets—what you would really love is a lingerie-themed party where all the guests bring satin teddies and camisoles and robes!

chapter 11

Looking and Feeling Gorgeous on Your Wedding Day

Your wedding day, and the months and weeks leading up to it, will *not* be special if you become a bridal basket case and get completely run down by the many stresses inherent in the whole wedding planning process. From dealing with difficult people to having a to-do list that burns out your Blackberry, to watching your budget soar to handling the demands of your career while you're running on empty; the many faces of wedding stress can sap all the enjoyment out of the whole thing. All of this stress is the opposite of *special*.

So in this section, you'll get a few needed reminders on how to release some of the tensions and care for yourself, be at your best, and look your best for the wedding day. You'll enjoy it so much more if you're balanced and happy.

Zapping Stress

324. Schedule regular relaxation into your busy schedule. The closer the wedding day comes, the more stress you'll encounter, so make those appointments for regular massages, manicures, and pedicures. You'll walk in there with your shoulders up to your ears, then slowly melt into a more relaxed state and leave feeling refreshed, which is the best state to be in when you're planning your wedding.

325. Step out of the bridal zone once in a while. Your entire world shouldn't be about being a bride, so make a conscious choice to put that bridal magazine down and step out as the person you are, the person you were before you got the ring. Make time for your regular interests, activities, and clubs. In addition to relaxing you, surveys show that relationships in which both partners maintain their own separate interests are much stronger than those where the couple merges into one entity. So consider your time at the book club, dance class, or volunteering at the animal shelter to be a wise investment in your future together.

326. Schedule regular meetings for coffee or drinks with your friends, where you can let loose and laugh, talking about anything other than the wedding. Again, studies show that regularly interacting with others and having a strong social circle make you a healthier and happier person. Plus, who wants to lose touch with their friends? Connect often, and laugh often. That, too, is a big mood-booster for your wedding planning reserves.

327. Schedule time for the two of you as a couple. This is so important, since many grooms become shocked (and, okay, a little scared) at how intense their brides can get over the wedding plans and their bossy mothers and their bratty sisters. Set up dates with your man, or just plan to spend Sunday mornings reading the paper, cuddling, having breakfast, and enjoying each other's company.

328. Exercise. It's the best stress reliever. Stick to your regular workout plan, or indulge in a gym membership and take a new class. Go for a walk, pop in a yoga DVD, or just crank up the music in your living room and dance. Anything that gets your blood pumping is a plus, and as a bonus, you're working toward looking fabulous in your wedding dress.

329. Write it down. Sometimes wedding stress can be relieved through a pen. Start a journal to get all of your thoughts and concerns out of your head and onto paper. Especially when the stress picks up and you're lying awake at night, often the best thing you can do is release your thoughts onto the page, then let yourself off the hook about worrying. You can review your notes tomorrow and make a plan of action when the sun has risen. Journaling is a top way to process all the questions and concerns you might have, de-stressing you so that your wedding planning time will be more special as a whole.

330. Make time for sleep. Without it, you won't be very efficient, and you will likely get ill if your body and spirit run down. Don't even think about telling yourself, "Who has time for sleep?" You don't have time *not* to sleep—not if you want to enjoy planning your wedding. Lack of sleep is an epidemic in this country, and it can cause your brain to get foggy. Not a special feeling. So practice smart sleep methods: go to bed a bit earlier than usual, at the same time every night, unwind before bed, don't do any work in bed, and look into aromatherapy options for relaxation. Lavender can help promote sleep, so look for a lavender linen mist to spritz on your sheets. Then it's off to sleep for you.

331. Nourish yourself. Coffee and a doughnut on the run will eventually sap your energy, so look at your diet and make a conscious effort to eat nutritious foods that make you feel healthier. Read up on healthy diet practices, or just put into effect the wise food choices you read about in magazines every month. Since you're so distracted with the wedding, you might be apt to grab unhealthy snacks. Bite this bad habit by shopping for healthier snacks and making sure your meals are balanced. Brides especially are in danger of running on empty due to pre-wedding diets, so watch out for restrictions and use good nutrition smarts.

332. Stay hydrated. Carry that tall bottle of water with you wherever you go to stay well hydrated, have more energy, and keep your skin and hair in good shape. Being hydrated actually helps you stay more alert and mentally sharp, so keep swigging that water.

333. Indulge in some pampering. Go to a day spa once a month for the works. Try something new, like a hydrating conditioner for your hair, a seaweed wrap, a hot rock massage, or a hydrating facial. Spas have incredible new offerings, so treat yourself like a princess and sign on.

334. The same goes for your *groom*. Men are increasingly going to day spas and salons to have their skin treated, their hair cut, and some waxing done. Encourage your guy to join the ranks of his fellow men who are sitting in the stylist's chair for some indulging, and perhaps even a "sports manicure" for the big day.

335. In advance of the wedding, you might want to try laser hair removal, which many women call a big blessing. Or get regular facials to improve the look and feel of your skin.

336. Have your hair professionally "practice-styled" for the wedding. This way-in-advance session with a stylist can show you how you'll really look with a dramatic updo as opposed to having your hair set in "sexy bedhead" style. If you don't already have a regular hairstylist you trust for your most important hairdo, make appointments with several. Choose the one who captures your ideal look and has the personality you want to deal with on the morning of your wedding.

337. Have your makeup professionally done in a practice session and then again on the wedding day. Experts know just how to apply makeup that looks great in real life and also shows up best in wedding photographs.

338. Rather than planning to go to a salon on the morning of the wedding, book a stylist and makeup artist to come to your home or hotel room on the morning of the wedding. You'll be in more relaxed surroundings, and there's something very special in a Hollywood sense about having stylists come to *you*.

339. Tan smartly. Rather than bake in a tanning booth or risk those UV rays out on the beach, have a professional apply sunless self-tanner evenly to your body.

340. Try a new tan application process, in which the color is sprayed on evenly.

341. Have your hair color or highlighting done professionally as well, unless you've been doing your own color for years and trust your own hand better than anyone else's. You might want to have your hair highlighted months and months before the wedding to be sure the new look would be for you, and then plan with the stylist when the perfect time would be for your wedding day highlighting touch-ups.

342. Splurge a little and have your eyebrows professionally shaped. Experts say this one grooming step has the effect of a facelift, changing the look of your face, enhancing the look of your eyes, and giving you a more polished look.

343. Pamper your skin. Use a great moisturizer, and consider getting your hands and feet paraffin-dipped for a baby-smooth softness.

344. Find a great fragrance. Experiment with several different kinds of scents before the wedding day, and choose the one that says "I am a Bride."

345. Play with several styles. Tear out pictures from magazines, and go to the bookstore to buy magazines that feature nothing but hundreds of hairstyles.

346. Make your hair a sculpture. Today's hairstylists can sweep up your hair into ringlets or chignons, making your mane an architectural masterpiece and a true vision on your wedding day.

347. Add some extra hair to your own. Ask your stylist to find or create a hairpiece that matches your exact hair color. You can find clip-on chignons, long lengths of real hair for an elegant ponytail, braided strips to wrap around a ponytail or chignon, poufy wisps of hair that will make a high and tight ponytail of shorter hair stand out and grab attention.

348. Mix hairstyles. A sideways French braid across the crown of your head can give way to a looser gathering of curls in the back. Such mix-and-match hair styles are hot right now, and give the bride something special for her wedding-day look.

On the Day

349. Appoint a bridesmaid or friend to give you the heads-up if your hair or makeup needs refreshing during the wedding day.

350. Don't forget to look special at *all* of your wedding events. Have your hair done for the rehearsal dinner, even if it's just a swishy blowout or straightening. It's not just the wedding day where you'll be the focus of attention.

351. Bring along (or have a friend bring along) a tote filled with fixer-uppers like pressed powder, lip gloss, eyeliner, hair spray, nail file, eyeliner, tissues, contact lens solution, pain relievers, facial tissues, and anything else you'll need.

352. Throw some breath mints into your fixer-upper kit. You'll need them on the wedding day!

353. Make sure you eat on the morning of the wedding. You'll need to have something in your stomach to give you energy and keep you from feeling dizzy or faint.

Beauty Regimes

354. Look what all the other brides are doing! *Wedding-Bells* magazine's survey turned over these fun stats for the bride's big day:

- 56 percent will whiten their teeth
- 14 percent will try a sunless tanner
- 79 percent will wear a designer fragrance on their wedding day
- 77 percent will wear high-end department store cosmetics on their wedding day
- 22 percent of eyeglass wearers will wear contacts on their wedding day
- 24 percent will don a new hair color for their wedding day
- 53 percent will use products that offer a "shimmering" effect, such as body creams and moisturizers
- 64 percent will experiment with new cosmetics and fragrances before their big day

chapter 12

Dressing Your Men

Your groom and his men will also look their best on the wedding day, whether dressed to kill in smart black tuxedoes, or dressed down in khaki pants and crisp white shirts for a beach wedding or Nantucket-style clambake. This section is where your men, including the dads, will pull their look together with some special flair.

355. For the ins and outs of choosing the right tuxedo and formalwear designs for the appropriate formality and style of your wedding, I encourage you to visit the following bridal websites:

www.bridalguide.com

www.brides.com

www.modernbride.com

www.theknot.com

www.weddingchannel.com

356. Choose from the latest and hottest male formalwear fashions by visiting rental websites and the sites for top designers. Collect images and let your groom know which way you're leaning. Since you're likely to be more well read on matching the style of tuxedo to the formality level of your wedding, make sure you explain to your groom the rules about tuxedoes with tails, white-tie options, and other style requirements.

357. All-white ties and vests paired with a black or gray tuxedo will make your groom stand out from the pack of black-tied men.

358. Go for the colored vests and ties, but be sure the shade you choose doesn't have a resonance of "Welcome to the Prom."

359. Formal and elegant black and white usually works best, unless you can find a great *patterned* black or gray set of tie and cummerbund or vest. Check out the many, many designs out there.

360. Try fun theme designs like wine bottles or anchors (if those designs match the theme of your wedding), checks, diamonds, stripes, and other sophisticated patterns.

361. An exception is great colors in wine tones, deep greens, and navies. It's those lilac vests that call back to the prom.

362. Layer up your man with a great vest and tie, or go Euro-glam with a cravat and vest worn over a wing-collar shirt.

363. Gray is the new black, especially if you can find a gray tux in a slightly shinier fabric. This elegant look is right off the runways and works well for a formal wedding. Choose a matching gray tie for the best look.

364. There's also something to be said about the new lines of midnight blue tuxedoes, for the men who want something different from black, but still want to look formal. Make sure it's a deep, deep navy and that the tie and vest match well. Clashing navies is a fashion war you don't want. Outfit your women in navy as well, or a slightly lighter shade of blue, and it's a gorgeous look for your group pictures.

365. Don't underestimate the look of a narrowly striped vest to make a statement on a black, gray, or navy tuxedo. As an added bonus, the guys will find that the stripes are more slimming, elongating their torsos and making them look taller.

366. Long ties are in—even for formal looks. Consider putting just your groom in this look to set him apart, and you're borrowing a celebrity style right off the red carpet.

367. The cravat is a high-style form of tie that will set your men apart from all groomsmen before them. Look into this style and see if its English-manor flavor works for you.

368. Look for open-backed vests as a better choice than full-backed vests. These attach-at-the-back styles leave the men less restricted, a bit cooler, and they're also more comfortable for the larger guys.

369. For informal weddings, including beach and outdoor weddings, let the guys relax by having them wear khaki pants and a crisp white button-down shirt. This clean look works well for laid-back weddings, and it makes for truly enduring pictures to display in your home.

Shoes and Accessories

370. Have all of your men wear the same style of shoe. Rentals are a great option, but the men's girlfriends and wives will thank you for encouraging them to go out and buy a new pair of good dress shoes.

371. The shoes always match the pants. With black tuxedoes or suits, it has to be black patent leather shoes. If the men are wearing ivory, which is a big color for summer weddings, then they'll need to rent ivory shoes to match. Check out men's formalwear websites (like www.afterhours.com) or talk to the men's fashion consultant to decide between traditional tie-up or sleek black slip-on shoes for men, according to the latest fashion trends.

372. At informal weddings, the men can wear loafers, or go barefoot with the rest of the guests on the beach.

373. Make *sure* the men know they are to wear dark formal socks with their dark shoes! Uniformity is a big thing with your men's look, so avoid the white sock phenomenon and leave a few extra pairs of dress black socks where the men will prepare for the big day.

374. For a sentimental accessory, give your groom a watch as a wedding gift, or as an earlier anniversary or birthday gift so he can wear it at your wedding.

375. Look at a wide range of cufflinks and button covers. You'll find jeweled styles with a bit of flash, geometrical designs, onyx, icons, and colored accessories to buy or rent.

What Your Guests Should Wear

376.

Be sure that your invitations convey to male guests what they are expected to wear to your wedding. If, for instance, you've planned a black-tie wedding, all of the men on your list need to know that they are to rent tuxedoes for your ultra-formal affair. Here's a primer on how to word it correctly in just this one simple phrase either on the bottom of the invitation or on a simple card insert in the invitation packet.

- "Black Tie Invited" means you may wear a tuxedo if you choose to, but it's not mandatory.
- "Black Tie Preferred" means we'd really like you to wear a tuxedo, so please make every effort.
- "Black Tie" means this is a formal wedding. Everyone else will be in tuxedoes, so please go rent one.
- "White Tie" or "Full Dress" means white tie, ultra-formal tuxedoes are mandatory.

chapter 13

Dressing Up the Children

For weddings, kids in the bridal party come in two types: the ones who love to play "dress up" in front of the crowd and the ones who'll fight you kicking and screaming when you try to button up their outfits. It all depends on the individual child's temper, maturity level, and demeanor, and also on how well *you* do in choosing what they're going to wear for the big day. Done right, you can dress up those little angels to make a very special and adorable impression at the wedding.

Flower Girls

For this section, I spoke with Dina Alhadeff, a merchandiser for *Storybook Heirlooms* (www.storybook.com), my absolute favorite source for kids' wedding-day wear for the brightest and prettiest ideas in flower girl dresses. Following are some things that Dina recommends for a look that every flower girl will want to wear.

377. "Children at the wedding provide an element of story-book magic, bringing in a touch of whimsy in an event that can otherwise be more solemn than anything else. So make your flower girl dresses more magical and whimsical, something the child will feel like a little princess in."

378. "Brides of today have such wide choices when it comes to their flower girl dresses. In the past, the flower girl usually wore a simple white dress to somewhat match the bride, with an air of innocence added to the effect. Now, the dresses don't have to be white. Choose from a wide range of colors, either for the entire dress in full, or as special accents."

379. "Tie in the color of the bridesmaids' dresses either in the color of the bodice to the dress, a sash, appliqués, or a trim to the skirt."

380. "At Storybook, flower girls' dresses with colored *petals* within a tulle skirt are a pretty, delicate children's look that adds something special to an otherwise simple skirt."

381. "Silk flowers can be added to a flower girl dress design at the waist, at the back, at the shoulders, or on the trim of the dress. Choose from a rose, a dahlia, or other flowers."

382. "One color combination that's enormously popular for the little girls' dresses is a celadon and pink combination."

383. "Choose a beautiful fabric! Now, the little girls' dresses can be found in organza, tulle, satin, and silk dupioni for more of a styled look and indeed more comfort for the little girl wearing it."

384. "In fall or winter, look for rich velvets as your flower girls' dress style. A velvet bodice with a petal skirt is a picture-perfect look for the little girls, and you can go with any number of colors: blacks, reds, burgundies, navies, hunter green, etc."

385. "Hugely popular are velvet and organza dresses, such as with a rich burgundy velvet bodice and a dusty pink organza skirt. Add your choice color of flower to the waist."

386. "Another big choice for weddings where red is the main décor color, and perhaps the bridesmaids are wearing red, is to have your flower girl in a white dress with red rose petals set in the tulle."

387. "Look at our iridescent gowns with a stretch lace bodice and gossamer tulle, with faux pearl flower sprays at the waist."

388. "Very princessy are the Venice lace dresses of satin and tulle, with sheer, puffed sleeves."

Dresses for the Princesses

389. Visit www.storybook.com to get a great look at the prettiest styles of magical flower girls' dresses in the following categories:

- Ballerina dresses
- Cascade dresses
- Embroidered netting dresses
- Embroidered organdy dresses
- Embroidered dresses with rosettes
- Iced silk dresses
- Pastel stretch lace tops with tulle tea-length skirts
- Lacy satin dresses
- Linen and tulle gowns
- Faerie ribbon dresses with cap sleeves and a tulle cover over a taffeta skirt
- Satin cutwork dresses (you have to see the floral cutouts on these!)
- Silver satin dresses with rhinestones (amazing look if your maids are in silver metallic as well)
- Velvet taffeta dresses
- Scattered flowers dresses with floral and bead accents on the tulle skirt

390. "Tea length is traditional for most flower girls' dresses. It's a pretty look, and it allows more comfort in movement for the girl."

391. "Speaking of the magic and whimsy of a princessy flower girl dress, look at half or full petticoats for the girls to wear beneath their skirts. With that wonderful lift that adds pretty volume to skirts, it will look like your adorable little flower girl is floating into the room."

392. "Always avoid discomfort when choosing flower girls' outfits. Make sure the fabric is soft, not scratchy, and (very important!) that the label on the dress is made of satin…nothing that can be itchy on the wedding day."

393. "For the girls' shoes, ballet flats are making a comeback again after a few years of fading away. Now, countless brides are outfitting their little girls' feet for comfort, and getting back to that ballet whimsy of the little princess."

394. "A matching flower headband ties in the color of the dress, and finishes off your little girls' look with another touch of pretty."

395. "We've paired some of our more magical dresses with angel wings for when little girls want to play dress up. Consider letting your flower girls float into the room wearing their marabou-edged wings for that bit of fancy you're looking for!"

396. "Another great princess look is the faux diamond and pearl tiara that little girls love to wear, and it could be a very lovely match to your own tiara headpiece."

Ring Bearers

397. Of course, the little guys can style out in tuxedoes that match the men's style exactly, right down to the bow tie.

398. For a formal or semi-formal look, they can wear a black suit with a white shirt, and a little tie in a color that coordinates with the men's look.

399. For an informal or beach wedding, put the little guys in khaki pants with a white shirt, or even khaki shorts with the white shirt.

400. If the men will wear a navy blue blazer with their khakis, the ring bearer can wear the same (just until the ceremony and pictures are over with, and then that jacket's coming off!).

401. Have fun with the boys' accessories. Even if the men are in formal black tuxedoes, let the little guy stand out by putting him in a tie that matches the bridesmaids' dresses. Tell him that having a different color means he's the most special guy up there.

402. For shoes, consider having the boys' parents purchase black dress shoes or shoes that work with the look he'll be wearing for the day. Let parents know about discount shoe shops or sales to help them out with the price a little bit, but know that the kid's going to get multiple uses out of those shoes.

Special Ideas for Kids

403. Give the kids a special piece of jewelry to wear for the wedding day as your gift to them. It could be a simple silver heart locket, a diamond pendant, a charm bracelet, etc.

404. Give a special flower girl something special from you. Perhaps it could be *your* charm bracelet or heart locket from when you were a little girl.

405. Allow outgoing and charming ring-bearers to help seat guests at the reception.

406. Let the kids be the ones to introduce you into the room at the reception.

407. Have a special menu arranged at the rehearsal dinner and at the reception that includes kid-friendly foods such as burgers or mini burgers, personal pizzas, chicken fingers, and other foods kids love. The little ones aren't going to touch the raw seafood bar, and they'll need to be fed!

408. Arrange for separate child entertainment at the reception. Some enterprising couples arrange for the little ones to spend an hour at the reception, and then be led up to a hotel room or to a separate room in the building for a kids' party with movies on DVD and perhaps even a clown or entertainer hired for the party. Hire babysitters or childcare workers to keep an eye on the little ones at this separate location.

409. Make it a pajama party if the reception will last into the late-night hours. Ask parents to bring their kids' sleepover kits with pajamas and sleeping bags, and let the party for the little ones begin.

410. Have a lunchbox or backpack at their place setting for each child at the reception, filled with all kinds of handheld games, coloring books, dolls, and other toys to keep them occupied for the evening.

411. Play a song or two at the reception that kids love. It needn't be one of those syrupy, annoying songs from a kids' TV show, but rather something from *The Lion King*, *Shrek*, or other movies kids count among their favorites to get them out on the dance floor.

412. Have a separate bar set up at the reception for kids. It could hold pitchers of soda, juice, water, or punch, or you might have a server hired to keep the kids with drinks in hand (lucky guy!).

413. Rather than play "pass the spoon" or "whose birthday is closest to the wedding day" to decide which guest get to take home the centerpiece, make it a kid-centered game. Bring the kids out onto the dance floor, and have them pick names out of a hat or play for a guest of their choosing in a game of ring toss or musical chairs.

chapter 14

The Rings

The rings you exchange will remain as the everlasting symbols of your marriage commitment to one another. They'll be on your hand every day. So, right now, start thinking about ways to make these rings even *more* special to both of you.

414. Take a ring primer at any of the major bridal websites to learn more about the four Cs of diamonds (cut, clarity, carat, and color), as well as the makings of a great ring band and design elements. This information is also available at jewelers' stores and at many of the more popular jewelry websites, like the following:

American Gem Society: www.ags.org

Blue Nile: www.bluenile.com

Novell Design Studio: www.novelldesignstudio.com

Tiffany: www.tiffany.com

Zales: www.zales.com

A Diamond is Forever.com:
www.adiamondisforever.com

415. Design your own rings at the above ring sites, where you can choose the metal, stone or stones, any design you want for your bands, and the quality of the ring itself. Print out your desired ring design for your shopping trip at reputable ring shops.

416. Bring a printout of your desired ring designs to a jeweler to have them custom made for you.

417. For an artisan's touch, bring your ring printout to a metal jewelry designer along with the stones you wish for the artist to set into the rings.

418. Shop for ring stones separately at jeweler's centers or the diamond district of a big city. Many brides and grooms have found that while this isn't the most efficient means of getting a ring, since it does take some travel and deal-making, it often makes for a better deal on the individual stones you'll have set into your bands, which will be bought separately at the jeweler's. This stone-shopping trip is best if you bring along a friend who's in-the-know about fine jewelry, one who can answer some of your questions and advise you on which are truly the best-quality stones. An informed consumer is more often the happy consumer, and you'll walk out of there with your precious gems ready for setting.

419.

Try your luck at antique shops, where fantastically crafted Old World rings are waiting to be brought back to life. Some brides tell me that they love buying jewelry from antique shops, since they quite romantically imagine the great story behind each of these rings and necklaces. Could these be the treasures a long-ago suitor traveled to England for, in search of the perfect ring to win over the daughter of his family's rival? A ring with a story and a history adds a little something to the romance of your wedding day, even if you have to take some literary liberties in imagining a great tale for the piece. Regardless of your talent for a great ghost story, you'll find a wealth of great rings in antique stores. This, most importantly, includes amazing settings in which to place your newly bought stones. Jewelry experts always marvel over the amazing craftsmanship of early era rings. Considering that the kinds of laser-cutting machinery we have now didn't exist back then, it's amazing to think that those tiny, intricate swirls and etchings in a ring were done by hand so many years ago. That can be a one-of-a-kind ring design, at nowhere near what it costs to have a custom ring made today.

420. Look at heirloom jewelry, perhaps your grandmother's wedding ring, or your great-grandmother's ring. What could be more special than carrying on the legacy of your grandmother's supremely happy marriage, and honoring the women of your family, by wearing one of their treasured rings? Even better, this can become an heirloom ring for your own grand-daughter someday, adding generations of love to the symbol of the ring itself. You can't put a price on a sentiment like that.

421. Have diamonds or stones reset from a family member's ring or pendant into a completely new setting for a more modern, cleaner look at a fraction of the cost. One bride who inherited her grandmother's engagement ring found the setting to be too garish for her petite hand. One giant stone surrounded by six smaller stones was just too much flash for her. So she took the ring to a jeweler, had the one big stone used for her engagement ring, and then set the six smaller stones into her wedding band. She saved the setting for a future date, in case her kids would ever want to restore the grandmother's ring to its former glory. In the meantime, she's just saved her fiancé $9,000 by providing her own meaningful stones for her rings, and the couple used that money for their honeymoon (with plenty left over afterward to get the home computer system they wanted).

422. Go for a unique shape of diamond in your wedding band. Try tiny heart-shaped diamonds set into your band, or a collection of more square cushion-cut stones set into the channel setting. For a bit extra in specialty stones, you can get star-shaped brilliants, or even triangular diamonds placed into your settings for a more graphic look.

423. Go symbolic with the stones you arrange in your ring. A cluster of three diamonds, for example, could stand for your past, present, and future. You could choose six diamonds for the six years you've known one another, or eighteen diamond chips reaching all around the band itself to signify that you and your fiancé met when you were both eighteen years old. Again, having a "story" to your rings is what it's all about.

424. Choose a wedding band that is designed to fit with your engagement ring. Your band can, for instance, hold several stones in a channel setting, and then leave an indented gap where the stone from your engagement ring would fit into a groove while worn next to your wedding band. A perfect fit.

425. Look at the new styles of laser-cut rings. From scalloped edges to intricately cut lace designs, today's wedding rings are all about style and originality. Ask your jeweler to show you the fancy-cut styles of rings to see if you like their lacy appearance and the potential upkeep of grooved rings.

426. For men's rings, look at dual-metal rings, ones with both silver and gold in them to match any wardrobe look, any watch he wants to wear with it, any passage of his preferred jewelry styles.

427. If you do wish to buy ring sets, rather than choose the band you want and the wedding ring he wants, know that you can find matching wedding rings for a more unified look. Check out the offerings thoroughly. Today's ring designers have come a long way from the simple, rounded platinum band. Now, you can choose rings with unique diamond chip designs, geometrical levels to the rings—real works of art.

Sentimental Additions

428. Of course, you can make your wedding bands extra special by having senti-mental words or phrases engraved inside them, in an array of attractive fonts. Here's just a short list of possibilities:

- *Forever*
- *Now and Forever*
- *For Eternity*
- *I Love You*
- *My Best Friend*
- *Take My Hand*
- *Yours Forever*
- *Finally!*

You could also use:

- Your wedding date
- Your names and your wedding date
- Any nicknames you have for one another
- Your wedding date on one side, the day you first met on the other

429. Always go for comfort when looking for rings. A square-edged or sharp-edged ring will account for many pinches and snagged stockings down the road, so ask your jeweler for "comfort cut" rings, or some shaping to make the bands less edged.

chapter 15

Your Flowers

We'll talk much more in detail about flowers for your décor later in this book. For now, we're going to concentrate on how flowers can make your appearance on your wedding day even more special, even more bridal, and even more beautiful. From bouquets to a single flower in your hair, this is where you will choose the floral look that puts the finishing touch on your wedding-day style.

Bouquets

430. The traditional cascading bouquet is back, although not as dramatically sweeping as they were in the '80s when you could barely see the bride behind that draping of flowers and greenery. Look for a gentle curve instead.

431. Go traditional with a round or cascading "bridal" bouquet of white roses and stephanotis, perhaps lilies and other flowers that come right from the standard list of wedding day bouquets.

432. "Branch out," so to speak, by using flowers that aren't so traditionally bridal but still make a gorgeous bouquet, such as peonies and geraniums.

433. Build your bouquet out of family favorites, such as your grandmother's or mother's favorite flowers, along with your own. Some of the most popular flowers of this nature, reported by real life recent brides, are gardenias, peace roses, and orchids. Using such favorites makes your bouquet an extra special tribute to the special women in your life.

434. Make your bouquet a tribute to your relationship, by using red roses just like the ones he bought you on your first date, or the white orchids that were on the table the night he proposed, or a mix of the two. Your bouquet can be a tribute to your great start as a marrying couple.

435. Go natural, with a cluster of daisies and other garden-type flowers for a less formal wedding.

436. Go unique, with a gathering of six long-stemmed calla lilies tied with organza ribbon. The look is extremely elegant and extremely bridal.

437. Make the filler around your bouquet roses stand out by choosing flowering greens, even berry clusters, unique ferns, trailing jasmine, sweet peas, and other pretty pieces.

438. Look for unique petals to the flowers in your bouquet. Peonies, ranunculus, and peace roses have lovely scalloped edges and a tint of color at the outer edges in some varieties. This can make your bouquet "pop" visually and perhaps even require fewer flowers for a less expensive bouquet.

439. Make it handheld by choosing a swinging pomander bouquet, a look that's growing in popularity right now. Using a bunch of pretty flowers attached to a round or teardrop shaped ball of foam, your pomander can hang from a length of ribbon, a braid of corded silk, or even a string of pearls for a very special bridal look.

440. Adorn the flowers of your bouquet by having the florist push pearl-headed pins into the centers of each bloom. For smaller flowers like an all-stephanotis bouquet (very detailed, very bridal, and very pretty!) use one pearl pin per flower. For larger roses, use three to six.

441. Use pearl pins that are white, ivory, or even blush-colored.

442. Add some sparkle to your bouquet by having the florist attach crystals either in push-pin manner, or using lengths of crystals on clear plastic strings for that waterfall look.

443. Use netting or veiling as a backdrop to your bouquet. Especially if the netting has pearls embedded, this makes for a pretty bouquet filler and a dramatic look.

444. Using traditional ivy as the greenery for your bouquet hearkens back to the days when everything was about symbolism. Ivy is symbolic for long and lasting fidelity, so it could be a good luck charm for you to insert some fresh and lovely deep green ivy into your bouquet.

445. Get a look at the amazing types of flowers out there by stopping at an arboretum, an extensively stocked nursery, or a flower show, and take some notes on unique flowers that might be perfect for your wedding day look and colors.

446. Go with the colors of the season. Deep oranges and yellows, cinnamon colors, and burgundies are perfect for a fall wedding, for instance, while those bright reds are ideal for the winter holidays.

447. Go with all color! Forget the all-white bouquet. Today's brides are walking down the aisle holding bright red bouquets, deep purples, blush pinks, soft blues, bright and sunny yellows, and autumn oranges.

448. You won't even need a headpiece if you have your hair styled in a beautiful updo—whether chic and straight or curled and sculpted. You can keep it loose and flowing, with perfectly arranged tiny flowers pinned into your braids or curls. Look at small stephanotis, baby rosebuds, even mini daisies for the perfect hair accents.

449. Tuck one single flower behind your ear. It could be a fresh and outdoorsy daisy or an exotic lily. It all depends on your style of wedding, especially if you're having an outdoor beach wedding where that lily will make you look like an island beauty.

450. Tuck a row of daisies into the back curl of a French twist.

451. Use a floral clip to keep a low-gathered ponytail in place, with a blooming touch. Just take a regular white hair clip or rounded ponytail clip and glue on fresh flower buds shortly before the wedding. Florists can make these for you if you're not a fan of do-it-yourself projects.

452. Wear a delicate wreath of flowers resting on the crown of your head. Done well, and with the right mix of flower styles and colors, this look is amazing! And it will save you a fortune on a pricey headpiece.

453. Mix up tiny fresh flower pin-ins along with pearl pins or tiny crystal bead clips to accent your hairstyle.

454. If your gown will have color, such as a blush pink hem and accent to the train, carry that color scheme up into your hair with baby pink rosebuds adorning you.

Flowers Elsewhere

455. The new style in bridal blooms is the floral wrist bracelet. Significantly more delicate (and less prom-like) than the wrist corsage, this bracelet might consist of a dozen small flowers strung together on a length of satin ribbon, and tied on as the perfect bracelet to complete your floral-adorned look.

456. Attach small fresh flowers to the top strap of your shoes. If you'll wear a short skirt or one with a dramatic slit up the side, a little showing of flower on your strappy heels will make something even more special out of your flash of a little leg.

457. Attach a cluster of fresh flowers to your purse or handbag. Of course, you can use silk flowers for this as a lasting keepsake, but this is an option if you want to carry your floral touches out to your accessories.

458. Attach a cluster of fresh flowers as well to your "gift purse," or the embellished oversized satin bag where you and your groom will place any envelope gifts handed to you by your guests.

PART FOUR:

The Party of Your Lives

chapter 16

Setting the Scene

Part of the wedding fantasy is what your reception is going to look like: the style, the details, the feel, the look, the transformation of a plain room into your magical wedding ballroom with a sea of flowers and candles…a setting that takes your breath away. Here is where you'll start thinking about setting the scene for your own incredible celebration event.

Know Your Places

If you're like most couples, your reception won't take place in just one location. Most parties move locales from one spot to another, or even to several different areas as in the case of a traveling reception, so you will need to think about how you're going to decorate the following settings using the tips from this entire chapter.

459. If you've planned a short span of time between the end of your ceremony and the beginning of the cocktail hour, your guests might be led to the lounge or bar at the hotel or the reception locale to have their first glasses of wine for the evening. If this is the case, then arrange to have flowers or candles in your wedding colors set at each table, along with those napkins and matchbooks with your names printed on them.

460. The cocktail hour location might be a separate party room off the grand ballroom, or even an outdoor terrace. Set this area apart with a different décor theme from your ballroom, perhaps with flowers and candles in a lighter hue than those in your main reception area. If you're on an outdoor terrace, bring in potted trees or potted flowers, candles in hurricane lamps, anything that enhances the outdoor scenery. Bistro tables can be set with a different color of linens from those in the ballroom, and different, simpler centerpieces can be used as well. If you go with simpler décor for this area, it makes a great "lead-in" to the more dramatic décor touches you've created for your ballroom.

461. The reception hall location, such as the ballroom or grand tent, offers a wide palette of décor opportunities. Borrow from interior decorators the concept of breaking the large room into "stations," with each area set apart with individual décor to make them all work together for a larger picture. For example, the entryway can be accented with flowers on pedestals, the dance floor accented with light, and so on. Take a big, empty space and see how you can create a unique look for each area, each corner, even each windowsill.

462. Each stop of the traveling reception can be decorated in a unique style, with subtle cultural themes or color schemes setting them apart. Areas to consider are a flower-filled terrace area, a poolside seating area and bar, a dinner room, a cigar bar, and that transformed outdoor terrace for desserts.

463. Common areas, such as hallways between the cocktail hour room and the ballroom where guests might gather, sit on couches, mingle and flirt with one another, can be dotted with floral arrangements, garlands, etc.

464. Restrooms can be spruced up with floral arrangements on countertops, candles in safe glass hurricane vases, potpourri, and silver or crystal bowls filled with mints. Some restrooms boast a separate lounge area with plush seating, large mirrors, and great lighting for guests' primping needs. In this case, set out another floral arrangement, along with a basket of personal care items like blotting papers, safety pins, travel-size hairspray, etc.

465. Outdoor smoking areas, such as terraces and benched areas for your smoking guests, can be decorated with some great candles on the tables and small buckets filled with colored sand for an improvement over those overfilled ashtrays.

466. Pathways between the parking area and the ballroom or terrace, or between buildings, can be lit with lamps, strung with floral garlands, posted with arrow directions and wording in great, color-coordinated print (e.g., *"Jim and Sarah's wedding this way!"*).

467. The bridal lounge, that separate room where both you and your bridal party might enjoy a short portion of the cocktail hour alone in a more intimate setting before you join all of your guests, can be a target of your decorative eye. Accent it with flowers on pedestals or in centerpieces, luxurious linens on tables and slipcovers on chairs, great mood lighting, comfortable seating, even jazz music piped in to set the tone and make a great, visual, and auditory transition for you before the big party begins.

Note: keep in mind that we will handle table settings separately in Chapter 17.

Flowers

468. Your banquet and serving tables can be decorated with large floral arrangements.

469. Try using economical but pretty scattered vases filled with tightly bunched flowers, set on blocks or pedestals for a little bit of height.

470. Set out tiny flower bunches in bud vases, lit from above with perfectly aimed pin lights.

471. Add a little bit of definition to the corners of the room by placing large floral arrangements on rented pedestals.

472. Set up a portrait table on which you'll display the framed photos from your parents' and grandparents' weddings, your siblings' weddings, and your favorite pictures of you as a couple during the courtship time before your wedding day. You can place your bouquet on this table, rather than in front of you at the main table you'll be sitting at.

473. For a bit of an extra floral touch to any table in the reception room—from the buffet table to the cake table—sprinkle rose petals on the tablecloths. Go for white petals if your tablecloths will have color to them, or colored petals in a monochromatic or coordinated color scheme if the tablecloths will be white. It's a very bridal look for just a small investment.

474. Also a great look: use large glass bowls filled with multi-colored or monochromatic rose petals. Fluff up the rose petals so you don't need so many per bowl.

475. Hang pretty floral pomanders on any doorknobs in the room, the restroom door handle, even pull tabs for window shades.

476. Set potted flowers or vases on windowsills.

477. Bring in rented trees to give the room something extra special. From ficus to flowering trees, even lemon trees and orange trees—all strung with fairy lights—this extension of the great outdoors brings new life to any reception location.

478. Don't forget the ceiling. Garlands draping across the ceiling area, hanging floral arrangements or oversized pomanders, even flowers arranged in the chandeliers will draw the eye upward and transform your room.

Candles

479. If there's one design element that makes any space more "bridal," it's candles. With the lights in the room dimmed, candles at each table and on the buffet table give the space a luxurious, elegant quality.

480. Set candles in protective glass hurricane lamps if they will be placed anywhere near anything that could potentially be flammable.

481. Place pillar candles in groupings on pedestals in the corners of the room.

482. Use elaborate candelabras on tables, on mantels, and on windowsills (but not on windows with drapes).

483. Group pretty votives in glass holders by any couches or sitting areas where guests will gather.

484. Place a lineup of pretty votives in glass holders on the bar.

485. Set votives or larger candles in glass holders on the buffet table between serving platters. This arrangement can do much to add a greater sense of volume to the buffet table, making it look like you have more there.

486. If you don't want candles on your buffet table or near serving stations, line them up safely *behind* the serving platters as a backdrop. This works especially well if the wall behind the buffet table is mirrored and can reflect the flickering lights.

487. If a location's vaulted ceiling has the attraction of a candleholder chandelier, make use of it with color-coordinated pillar candles.

488. Line a mantel with greenery, flowers, and candles in glass holders. Very elegant and romantic, especially if your room features a working fireplace that can be lit for your reception.

Decorate the Fireplace

489. If your site *does* have a fireplace, but it's not a working fireplace, you can still make it an incredible effect in your room by setting up a gorgeous fireplace-set candle holder frame. These lovely dark or silver upright metal frames will sit inside the fireplace, holding a dozen or so candles in a beautiful curved or stacked setup. Invest in one for your site, and then take it home to use in your own fireplace after the big event!

490. Look at the opportunity to hang wall sconces, or use existing wall sconces, at your reception location. Today's gorgeous sconces for sale or rent come in elaborate metal designs, and some feature mirrored backdrops for safety and reflection of the light.

491. For outdoor settings, look at buying or creating luminarias, which are small treated bags (like traditional lunch bags) with decorative hole designs punched out, filled with sand, and then set out with a votive candle burning inside. You'll find these in party supply stores or online in a wide range of colors from pastels to whites to silvers and golds, and even hologram designs. Set these in a path on walkways, stairs, the tops of stone walls, a passage on the beach, or any safe location.

Candles

492. The world of candles is just incredible. You can choose from solid-colored to multi-hued, candles with embedded seashells, spiked with crystals, scented or unscented, shaped into sandcastles or any other shape you have in mind, and adorned with anything you can imagine. Selecting unique candles can make all the difference. Check www.illuminations.com or www.pier1.com for looks and ideas.

493. Lighting is one area where wedding design borrows from big-time special events like the Academy Awards after-parties. With an elaborate lighting setup, reception settings become *shows*. It's not just mood lighting anymore with dimmed room lights and spotlights and a disco ball on the dance floor. Now it's all about laser lights and special lighting effects.

494. One such lighting effect is called "gobo" lights, which is a term for a projection system where a metal disc or a series of metal discs are fabricated into a design, then placed in front of a light. The result is a projected image, such as your names in elaborate script projected onto:
• the dance floor
• the walls of your reception room
• the walls of your tent
• the outside wall of a nearby building when your wedding is outdoors

495. Other gobo light effects can make any surface look like the ocean, with a range of blue waves, with a glowing sunset behind it (as in, bring the beach sunset to you!). You could also use it to create an Italian countryside effect, an "under the sea" image or any other design you can dream up.

496. Gobo lights can also be used to project images onto pool surfaces or dance floors. At one Arabian Nights-themed wedding, the coordinator designed an intricate Moroccan carpet design projected by gobo lights onto the surface of the pool for the evening cocktail party. Just gorgeous. Talk to a lighting specialist or a wedding coordinator about any theme or worded image you might wish to have projected by gobo lights at your wedding.

497. Of course, the most popular look in reception lighting is strings of white fairy lights. Just think about the light-strung trees you've seen at Tavern on the Green in New York City. The trees are lit up with thousands of lights, giving it a magical quality.

498. String fairy lights in trees and throughout landscaping.

499. String fairy lights on fences surrounding yards or pools.

500. Lights can be strung on the perimeter of your tent.

501. Use fairy lights inside the tent as a draped design to create a virtual ceiling to the tent, either alone or in conjunction with draped fabric.

502. String lights along walkways to create "fences" to the parking lot or along the path to poolside.

503. Spotlights in the ballroom can be arranged to highlight the beautifully detailed, elaborate cake, which is a major focal point for any reception site.

504. Add spotlights to the food stations or buffet table.

505. Pinlights above each guest table give the effect of a quiet, intimate dining room, a great look for any location. You can arrange to have one pinlight shining on your centerpiece, or even individual pinlights over each guest's plate.

506. For a truly unique lighting experience, check out Floralyte, a wireless, disposable, water submersible, self-powered small lighting unit that can be placed in bunches into candleholders, vases, floral arrangements, balloon arrangements, even fishbowls for a "wow, how'd they do that?" effect. Check these out at www.smartlyte.com/floralyte.html.

507. Use light projected *through* fabrics, such as strings of fairy lights strung behind fabric or tulle drapings.

508. Project light behind tall, rectangular rice paper screens or inside design boxes.

509. Project light from behind any trees you've brought into the room, or to make the most of at an outdoor location.

510. You can use the full effect of any *existing* attraction at a reception site, such as a fountain, gazebo, even a nearby waterfall or pond. Just by installing or asking the manager to switch on great lighting, you bring the full effect to your affair—it's priceless décor for not a whole lot of money (if anything at all).

511. Want a very cool lighting effect? Check out Air Star's (www.airstar-light.com) lighted balloons. Huge circular balloons can be suspended above your reception's dance floor or even arranged into a space-enhancing balloon wall. These illuminated balloons can be found in a range of colors and designs, such as planets or glowing solid colors, and, of course, you can get bridal white or silver iridescent for an unforgettable lighting look.

Special Effects

512. Laser lights are the big thing for the party atmosphere after dinner. Consult with a lighting specialist to give your guests an amazing show on the dance floor.

513. To create a laser show without the lasers, cover the ceiling and walls of your space with either a holographic film or a draped holographic fabric (www.holowalls.com). When lights reflect off of the holographic surface, the space above becomes a veritable movie screen, filled with projected décor, shooting stars, anything you can dream of with a laser light show.

514. You can even request holographic effects for a 3-D experience.

515. Have plasma screen TVs set up around the room to display any footage or images you wish. Some couples choose an aquarium DVD to play over and over for effect.

516. Other couples with a flair for the golden age of movies might play screen classics like *Gone with the Wind, Casablanca,* and other great love stories (with the sound turned off, of course). Having several movies playing on plasma screens gives a great effect for the tone of your party.

517. Another option for plasma screen televisions or larger television screens is to open your reception with a video montage of the two of you, complete with soundtrack, edited together by an expert or friend. Opening with "the story of our relationship" is a terrific way to start the party off on the right foot, to honor you as a couple, and to thrill your guests.

518. Fireworks are a dramatic special effect to celebrate any wedding. For this reason, many couples marry on the Fourth of July when area fireworks will be visible from their well-chosen reception site, and others do some smart research to see if their town is planning their Fourth of July celebration (or Rose Festival celebration, or any other occasion marked with town fireworks) on another day of that weekend. Know now that some communities hold their fireworks displays a few days away from the actual Fourth so as not to compete with other nearby towns' bigger celebrations. You might be able to research this and choose July second or third for your wedding date.

519. You can hire licensed fireworks experts to shoot off fireworks in your honor. Just be sure to get all the permits and permissions you need, and hire reputable experts who are knowledgeable about safety and are familiar with the location where your wedding will be. (Note: at some weddings, couples were disappointed when the fireworks company refused to set off fireworks due to drought conditions, gusty winds, or nearby woods—too dangerous.)

520. Now you can hire special-effects experts to construct a water screen system and on-site water features just for your spectacularly special wedding reception. Visit www.miragewaterworks.com to get a look at the many possibilities, such as the holographic screen that appears to have projected images hovering in midair. Very twenty-first century!

521. Special-effects companies are showing off an electric tape that can be programmed to glow in a range of different colors. Just apply the tape in stripes, grids, or other designs on your walls, and let them glow alone or in tandem with a laser light show.

522. You can rent backdrops in any design, from an icicle-strewn winter wonderland to a grassy field to the Washington Monument if you'd like. Today's designer backdrops are borrowing from Broadway-style grandeur, if not a Disney-esque attention to artwork perfection, providing you with a theme backdrop for your party. Choose from designs to colors, landmarks to nature scenes, even colors with geometric designs for a modern look.

Tents

523. Today's rent-a-tents have come a long way since the early days when you got a white square structure or a striped circus tent. Now, with modular tubing construction, tent experts can create shaped tents that make the most out of any landscape, even those with trees in the middle of them. Just build the tent *around* the tree.

524. Look for tents with built-in breeze-ways—part of their walls or the entrance should be netted to allow breezes to move through without straining the wall.

525. Look for tents with see-through ceilings to get a look at the stars.

526. Tent designers can install a top-quality parquet or tiled floor for your entire area under the tent. Look at the many different styles of flooring, from colored to white to sparkly to traditional black-and-white checked.

527. Look for tents with great design elements, such as scalloped tent liners, fabric draping, clear covered windows, archways, and other architectural additions.

528. Lay a walkway to your tent. Again, it could be rented flooring or it could be a homemade, elevated wooden walkway that you've covered with artificial grass or another great walkway material.

529. Have a separate tent for your restrooms, with a draped section for primping, mirrors, and good lighting.

Seating

530. The tables themselves can be a great attraction, and provide a wonderful, unique look to your reception room. Instead of those traditional eight-person round tables, why not go with the trend and arrange several long family-style tables that will seat sixteen to twenty? It creates a Thanksgiving-style celebration when more people are seated together.

531. Choose square or rectangular tables to fit your guests more comfortably than trying to arrange eight-seater tables. Experts say these square tables facilitate conversation between guests much better than round tables, too.

532. For a unique element and a great way to use floor space in your room, choose several different shapes and sizes of tables, such as rounds for the tables next to the dance floor, and rectangles for other tables in the room.

533. Mix up his side and her side. It used to be that the guest tables were divided down the middle, the bride's family was seated to the left of the dance floor and the groom's to the right. Now it's far better for family inclusion and mingling to intersperse tables and get all of your family and friends blended together.

534. Outside of the guest tables, perhaps at the cocktail hour, consider renting two-seater bistro tables for guests to enjoy some alone time.

535. Borrow from wedding coordinators who have done lounge-style parties and Moroccan theme parties: set out long, luxurious couches in rich jewel colors for guests to gather on, with plenty of fluffy pillows. This is great for the cocktail hour or the after-party.

536. At an outdoor wedding, provide some unique seating with bench swings, clustered beach lounge chairs, or even a few hammocks strung up between trees. Cozy couples can wander off hand in hand and swing in the evening breeze as *Summer Wind* is playing for the party.

537. At some outdoor weddings, bonfires and campfires with log seating dot the open-field landscape of the party. As the sun sinks on the horizon, groupings of guests or couples who have hit it off can sit by the fire and talk. Always use safety with this idea. Provide a wide stone perimeter around the fire to keep guests with long skirts from being in danger of getting too close.

Theme Décor

538. As an example of working a room's décor, consider the holiday-themed wedding: ice sculptures, clear crystal "icicle" candleholders, old-fashioned sleds and toboggans positioned as décor around the room, metallic or beaded snowflakes hanging from the ceiling, a dance floor designed to look like ice...

539. For a moon and stars-themed party, have glow-in-the-dark stars placed on the ceiling or the walls, project images of the universe or planets, or have a gobo light effect with a shooting star and your names. Decorate in deep blues or metallics. Give out star charts or books and CD-ROMs about constellations as wedding favors. Have a high-powered telescope by a window providing a great view of the night sky—and provide a star chart for that date that lets guests know which stars and planets are visible and where.

Work in the elements of your chosen theme, and don't be afraid to get creative with it! Almost anything can be rented these days!

chapter 17

Setting the Tables

I've devoted an entire chapter to this topic, since it's one of the areas where wedding planning has gotten incredibly diverse and where couples are focusing a lot of their attention. After all, the table is where guests spend a good portion of their time during the wedding (at least when they're not out on the dance floor!) and it's where they get an up-close and personal view of you and your tastes in wedding finery. Read on to get some new tips on setting your tables in style.

Place Settings

540. Look beyond the plain white china dishes shown to you by any hotel ballroom or restaurant. As their basic package, they'll let you use their ho-hum plates for nothing, showing you their standard place settings. You can do better than that.

541. Today, the look in place settings is all about being *unique*. That means plates and chargers with shining colored rims in a matching deep blue or red or silver, any color you could want.

542. Select floral patterns on the outside edges of the plates, or across the entire plate.

543. Bold gold patterns in standout swirls and geometric designs make your plates a piece of artwork.

544. Couples with big budgets are arranging to have their plates monogrammed with their entwined first and last name initials.

545. Some of the more elaborate rental agencies have designed plates with just the first letter of your new last name. They have every letter of the alphabet in stock. Check to see if you love the style.

546. Rental agencies report in that the new hot look in rented chinaware, chargers, and even serving platters is *square*. Couples with a vision are skipping the traditional round plates to have a little something different at each guests' place setting.

547. Look into other shapes, as well: ovals, octagons, even triangular plates are all making a big showing at today's special weddings.

548. Mix and match plate colors on each table. Make every other plate white and every other plate a deep navy blue, for instance, to give the table settings some pattern.

549. Similarly, have one smaller patterned plate set atop a larger solid-color plate for great effect.

550. Clear glass plates are also all the rage, including clear glass serving platters. These might be plain and unadorned, or they might have a wonderful design ingrained, such as a spiral, maze, or geometric shapes and accents.

551. Pearl-edged plates are also rising in popularity. While not real pearl, the raised "bumps" give a lovely bridal look to the table setting.

552. Gold plates are a hot look right now, so mix up shapes and go with gold platters.

553. Silver and copper are also hot, with the metallic look very "in" for daytime to evening.

554. Pearlized, clouded plates rimmed in color or metallic are a dreamy way to set your table, coordinating with your chosen color scheme.

555. For an outdoor wedding or cocktail reception, look for specially designed plates that have a great, handy feature: a cut-out slot built right into the plate that will actually hold their wine glass while guests enjoy the *hors d'oeuvres*.

Glasses

556. Look for wine, water, and champagne glasses with a unique stem: perhaps a braid effect, a square chunky design, or a thick circular stem.

557. The big new look is colored rims for all your table glasses. Look for deep colors to match your tablecloth and plates, or silver-, gold-, or copper-rimmed glasses.

558. Glasses don't have to be clear. Look at pearlized frosted glasses.

559. Hued glasses in pastels and brights can add just the right amount of color to your tables.

560. Choose funky martini glasses in color or with a zigzag stem.

561. Have a different set of glasses at the cocktail hour. Couples in the know said they used colored red glasses and martini glasses for their fun fiesta cocktail parties, and then switched to classic crystal for the more elegant reception. Making the switch conveys the change in tone for the party's stages.

562. At the bar, offer those terrific stemless vodka shot glasses that are shaped like ice cream cones and rest in a small dish of ice chips—very snazzy.

563. Look at more tubular shot glasses and soda glasses. These thinner, taller glasses are stylish for any drink.

564. Visit www.crateandbarrel.com for a look at more casual styles of barware for your less formal party. Some designs feature shaded or colored stems, air bubbles left in the foot of the glass, even cut-outs in the stem itself.

565. If kids will attend the reception, be sure to stock child-friendly glasses in sturdy, colorful plastics (the best ones don't look like plastic at all!) or glasses with good finger-grip designs.

Linens

566. No more plain polyester tablecloths in a range of twelve basic colors or a concerned mother at your side urging you to go with the plain white! Now, it's all about color and style with table linens, so go for great colors: pastels, bright navies, greens, and even reds work for elegant parties, and brights like fuschia, yellow, and orange are perfect for daytime summer weddings.

567. Work two colors into your table linens by setting the table first with one color, such as a bright or deep plum, and then laying a color-coordinating smaller tablecloth over it so that both colors show. Your designer will know just how to drape them for optimum color exposure.

568. Mix solids with sheers. Place a solid-color table-cloth on your table— perhaps a deep blue or blush pink—and then cover it with a separate full or partial tablecloth that is sheer, such as a "barely there" shade of silver or white. This translucent overlay gives a lovely softening of the original color, and it adds depth and dimension to your table. This one simple overlay gives the table a shimmering, ethereal glow and the perfect coordination of colors to show off your place settings and centerpiece elements.

569. A colored runner can be laid across the length of the table, giving a lovely wide stripe of color on which to lay centerpieces.

570. Use shimmery fabrics for table-cloths. They'll catch and reflect the great lighting of the room, making the entire table sparkle and glow.

571. Fabrics with great designs woven into them make for terrific bridal tables. While the design might not be too apparent, a closer inspection will reveal a delicate pattern of hearts or flowers in just a shade or two darker than the background. Elegant.

572. Look at fabrics that are fabulous to the touch. Silk dupioni is the fabric of choice for that smooth feeling and fabulous shine.

573. Look at damasks and jacquards as well for some texture and design.

574. Ivory and gold linen combinations are big for weddings right now, providing a bridal look mixed with a bit of royalty.

575. Lace is still hot for weddings, especially as an overlay to a wonderfully colored tablecloth, or even a matching ivory.

576. A sparkly organza tablecloth reflects the same style and movement of the bridesmaids' dresses.

577. For a classic, old-fashioned wedding look, check out a Battenberg lace cutout fabric placed over white taffeta moiré. You can't get much more bridal than this.

578. As an overlay, look at a shirred eyelet lace draped over a colored table-cloth, gathered up at four to six points for effect.

579. In response to more and more couples designing their weddings with a natural look, sage green is growing incredibly in the ranks of rental fabrics. Look at the soft green colors, accented by deeper greens, whites, and pinks.

580. For tabletops and chair backs, look at sashes and tassels in matching fabrics, shinier silks, moirés, taffetas, organzas, satins, and tissue lamé for some sparkle.

581. Decorate the chairs with well-fitted slipcovers that you can rent along with your other table linens. Designs include full-length chair covers with a sash that ties at the back of the chair.

582. Something a little bit new and streamlined, called Sculptware (www.sculptwareonline.com), is made from a stretchy fabric and fits like a glove over any chair. No dangling hems to worry about tucking under the chair, no guests tripping over chair slipcovers during the conga line!

583. Of course, you'll look at napkins in a coordinating color to match or complement in the tablecloth. Go for a shade lighter than the tablecloth.

584. Consider adding some design to the napkins themselves. It could be a swirl or a single border around the outside edge of the napkin, but it looks lovely as an accent when folded for presentation.

585. Monogrammed napkins are the essence of style, so look at renting single-initial monogrammed napkins, or invest in having them made for your reception.

586. For the cake table, choose a shiny, beaded fabric if your cake will be a traditional white or ivory cake with a beaded icing design. Matching the pearl look to your fabric will make your cake look more glorious.

The Tables Themselves

587. Check out clear acrylic or glass-topped tables at your rental agent. Designers are showing these tables, covered with a translucent tablecloth and lit from *below* by stationary light boxes for a focused glow coming up the center of the tables.

588. Fun accents for your cocktail party are the new, rental tables shaped like martini glasses, complete with an oversized olive resting at the base where the "glass" meets the "stem" of the table (www.villagecraft.biz).

Centerpieces

589. Floral centerpieces are the traditional choice for wedding receptions, and some can be truly elaborate, lifted up onto high pedestals so that guests have a chance to see each other across the table. Brenda K. Maynard, General Manager of Party Plus in Atlanta (www.partyplusatlanta.com), suggests a unique option: "Use silver coffee pots filled with old-fashioned roses."

590. Another popular option for floral centerpieces is placing them in the center of high candelabras with pillar or taper candles on the outside edges surrounding the floral design.

591. A new look in floral centerpieces is incorporating fruit, such as lemons or limes, for some natural color to go with your wedding colors.

592. Nuts, figs, and berry branches can also round out the natural look surrounded by fresh flowers.

593. Flowering branches are also on the rise, giving floral centerpieces some added height, dimension, and drama—and for all that extra material, they're surprisingly inexpensive!

594. A tight cluster of calla lilies in a tall, thin vase is very dramatic and elegant—simplicity at its best. Calla varieties come in white, a range of green hues, and even burgundy (called "cabernet").

595. Another option is a simple glass or crystal bowl, filled with water and holding a single gardenia. Surround the bowl with votive candles and perhaps a sprinkling of rose petals, and you have the perfect, stylish centerpiece.

596. For a bright look that adds to the ambience, choose large single pillar candles in your choice of color.

597. Groupings of pillar candles in different heights is another great look.

598. Place pillar candles on a circular colored platter, such as a lavender platter, to match your floral design.

599. Use a gold or silver platter to coordinate with the cutlery on the table and bring out a rich color scheme.

600. A red platter can work with your red-and-white theme.

601. Use a stylish black platter to work with your city-chic reception theme.

602. A geometrically shaped platter, like a square or an oval, a triangle, or even a wavy platter can add a great design element.

603. A mirror, either rectangular or circular, will reflect the flickering candlelight.

604. Center your tables with a thick grouping of votives in glass holders, in one color tone, or mixed to coordinate.

605. Center your tables with a low glass vase holding a tight cluster of peonies or ranunculus with bright greenery for a clean, fresh look.

606. Stick something into your floral arrangements, such as those glowing self-contained lights.

607. Add a Mardi Gras mask for a theme wedding.

608. A pinwheel can be added for whimsical outdoor weddings.

609. Any number of fun, seasonal, or theme-oriented stand-up objects would make great additions to your floral arrangements.

610. For beach weddings, center your tables with pails of sand with a starfish and a tiny sand shovel sticking out.

611. Center your tables with a molded sand-castle that looks like it's made out of sand, but is actually plaster.

612. Use a fishbowl containing live gold-fish and colored rocks at the bottom. (Just don't use this idea if it will be hot outside, or the fish will literally poach in the sun.)

613. Have a sand pail filled with enough brightly-colored pinwheels for each guest at the table.

614. A basket of daisies creates a natural look (and very inexpensive, too!).

615. The centers of your tables could be functional rather than decorative with a lavish display of bread in several breadbaskets moved from the buffet table to the guests' tables. Set out various spreads, olive oils, and tapenades to make it a treat.

616. Another functional centerpiece for your tables could be a basket of differently colored tortilla chips, along with salsa, guacamole, and bean dipping sauces.

617. Several stand-up containers holding breadsticks and grissini also make for an inviting table center.

618. Pitchers of brightly colored drinks, such as sangria or lemonade, with plenty of fruit slices floating in them, also center the table attractively.

619. Go natural with baskets piled high with fruits: lemons, limes, oranges, kiwis, or pomegranates in the fall.

620. A big, carved pumpkin is perfect for an autumn wedding.

621. A collection of unique and shapely gourds and mini pumpkins can become centerpieces for an autumn wedding.

622. Fill a silver bowl with beautiful holiday ornaments for a winter holiday wedding, with the ornaments indicated as guests' take-home favors.

623. Also doubling as favors are potted flowering plants.

624. You can also use potted herbs as a centerpiece that doubles as a favor.

625. Cactus plants are great for a desert-themed wedding.

626. A favorite idea of mine is to use mini bonsai trees.

627. Another favorite: mini bamboo shoots arranged in tiny planters. Bamboo is a symbol of good luck, so that's a great centerpiece as well as a great favor.

628. Place a single rose on the place setting of each guest as their welcome and their take-home favor.

629. Follow suit with a bunch of tulips or daisies, the stems of each bunch wrapped with some satin or tulle ribbon.

630. Have a printed "thank you for being here" note placed at each setting. You can print these up easily on plain or bordered post-card-sized papers using your home computer, and accent them with a color-coordinated ribbon attached at the top.

631. Some couples who have printed up these thank-you notes use greeting card papers (available at office supply stores) and include a full color picture of them on the front cover of the note.

632. Print up place cards using your home computer or use your great hand-writing, with every guest's name spelled correctly!

633. Instead of numbering your guest tables, which can rankle some guests' egos, name your tables according to the theme of your wedding. If, for instance, you're holding an Italian, family-style wedding, name each table after a town in Italy, or after an Italian artist or cultural icon.

634. If your wedding doesn't have a theme, use a favorite interest of yours instead to make it more personalized. One couple who loved wines and had visited many wineries during their years together named their tables after their favorite kinds of wines: Merlot, Shiraz, Cabernet, etc.

635. Provide a disposable camera at each table for guests to use as they snap candids of the fun you're missing at their table while you're off shaking hands and accepting congratulations.

636. At the exit, place a large basket by the door with a visible note for guests to deposit the disposable cameras in the basket for developing. Without ease of drop-off, some guests could take those cameras home with them.

Smart Guest Placement

637. Instead of grouping cousins with cousins and friends with friends, get a little bit more creative. If you know your groom's cousin would really hit it off with your co-workers, seat them at the same fun table.

638. The same goes for singles. Put your friends with his friends and see if anyone hits it off.

639. Seat the kids at one table, right next to their parents' table for an easy care-taking situation.

640. Seat family friends together, paired by their mutual interests, such as travel or art or cinema.

641. Icebreakers are a great idea at a wedding where you know most of the people won't know the others at their table. Print up question and answer cards, or set out fun trivia cards from a boxed board game, and allow guests to play at will.

chapter 18

A Menu to Savor

What makes a wedding truly special? Sure, the décor can impress your guests, and you're going to knock their socks off when you appear in your wedding gown like a dream, but it's the *food* that is the standout for any celebration. Great food on your menu can make your wedding a hit for all. In this section, you'll start thinking about what you can do to make the right choices in delectable cuisine.

642. Look through caterers' *regular* party menus as well as wedding fare menus to see what's possible that's not just traditional wedding party selections. Many times you'll discover more unique foods than the ones caterers have deemed appropriate for weddings.

643. Choose menu selections that have significance to you as a couple. For instance, if you made him beef teriyaki for the first meal you ever cooked for him, then adding that dish to your selection list brings a bit of nostalgia into your menu.

644. Do the same for your favorite dishes that you've enjoyed together on special dates, or just your usual Friday night quesadillas as an appetizer.

645. Choose foods that are a part of your heritage. Ethnic and cultural elements from both sides of families are all the rage right now in wedding menus, so scout your family's most traditional dishes (spanakopita, bratwurst and sauerkraut, flan, etc.) for a wedding menu that's a tribute to your backgrounds.

646. Choose foods that are a part of your family's favorite holidays, like your Mom's meatballs. They're not necessarily ethnic, but they bring back your best childhood memories and the comforts of home. Plus, it's a nice tribute to Mom or Grandma that these dishes are so meaningful to you.

647. Include some vegetarian and vegan selections so that your guests with special diets can partake of your choices. Ask your caterer for some guidance.

648. The same goes for kosher foods and any religious food requirements for the time of your wedding.

649. Ask your caterer to tell you all about the specialty foods that will be in season at the time of your wedding. From meats to seafood, certain times of the year bring an abundance of certain kinds of edibles that could be a good addition to your menu.

650. For seafood, know that the market changes all the time; certain fish and shellfish are hotter on the market depending on how the catch is. So leave your choice of fish *open* with your caterer until just before the wedding, when he or she can call to let you know that tilapia or blue claw crabs are perfect for your wedding time.

651. Ask your chef about food specialties. Right now, Australian lamb is big on the market and is expected to remain so for quite some time.

652. Build a multicultural menu. "Food fusion" is hot at all the most upscale restaurants in the big cities, so work with your chef or caterer to blend two diverse international cuisine styles. For instance, Asian and Cuban foods go amazingly well together—delicious seafood paired with rice and bean dishes.

653. Theme your cocktail party separately from your wedding. You could go with a fiesta-style cocktail hour, complete with mariachi band, and then move into the more formal traditional reception for the rest of the night.

654. Ask about great garnishing. Chefs can make a plain chicken breast into a work of art with just the right design of side dishes, sprinklings of spices and swirls of sauces, plus a tall tower of fried potato strings for height and drama.

655. As a garnishing art, your chef or caterer can design your monogram into your food presentations. Using stencils, they can sprinkle spices into the design of your new last initial, or pipe your initials onto petit fours. Let your food artist get creative with your monogram in your menu.

656. If you'll select unique foods for your menu, it's a wise idea to print up labels or cards that inform guests of the name of the dish, as well as the ingredients. With so many people allergic to peanuts or scallops or dairy, for instance, they'll need to know what's in each dish. It's a wise, considerate move that can open up food dish choices for guests who might otherwise be too leery to dig in.

The sample food choices on the following pages for passed *hors d'oeuvres* are from menus generously provided courtesy of the Westminster Hotel in Livingston, New Jersey (www.westminsterhotel.net), owned by the Glazier Group (www.theglaziergroup.com), with my thanks to celebrity chef David Walzog for his culinary genius.

657. Here are some ideas for hot *hors d'oeuvres* (select four):

- Moroccan lamb and date cigars with creamy harissa sauce
- Thai crab cakes with green curry sauce
- Almond-spinach phyllo triangles with pomegranate molasses
- Tandoori chicken skewers with minted yogurt sauce and mango chutney
- Ginger shrimp with honey glaze
- Sesame chicken with peanut sauce
- Pork empanadas with chocolate chili mole sauce
- Crispy shrimp wontons with sweet and spicy dipping sauce
- Rock shrimp lollipops with coconut dipping sauce
- Potato latkes with apple sauce and sour cream
- Smoked duck spring rolls with soy lemongrass dipping sauce
- Blue cornmeal chicken fingers with honey mustard sauce
- Lamb chop lollipop with sweet garlic purée

658. Following are some ideas for cold *hors d'oeuvres,* passed butler-style (select four):

- Smoked salmon napoleon with osetra caviar and crème fraîche
- Crostini trio with eggplant caviar, tomato-basil sauce, and tropical fruit

- Spicy beef carpaccio with basil and peanut sauce
- Chickpea hummus with lentil crisp
- Coriander-crusted lamb medallion with cumin aioli and toasted nan bread
- Saffron-scented jumbo shrimp with classic cocktail sauce
- Soy-lacquered duck breast with mango relish and wonton crisp
- Tuna tartare with slivered almonds and endive spear
- Pickled daikon and cucumber maki sushi roll with soy sauce
- Foie gras mousse with toasted croustade

Signature Stations

659. Here are some ideas for the various stations you might have placed around your cocktail party area:

Harvest Style

- Assorted vegetables with chef's selection of dipping sauces
- Roasted vegetable tartlets with melted cheese and herbs
- Grilled polenta triangles with smoked tomato aioli
- French cheese display with assorted flat breads, artisan breads, and water crackers

Soups (select two)

- Sweet potato soup with candied red peppers and basil-scented crème fraîche
- Wild mushroom soup with chestnut purée and white truffle oil
- Chickpea soup with chive oil
- Cream of potato soup
- Leek purée

Meat Carving Station

- Hand-carved, prime-aged strip loin
- Truffle-creamed spinach
- Garlic croustades

Salmon Station

- Soy-glazed whole baked salmon with pickled cucumbers
- Tequila-cured salmon
- Smoked Norwegian salmon
- Black bread, chopped egg, red onion
- Capers, parsley, and crème fraîche

Peking Duck Station

- Traditional Peking duck
- Moo shu pancake, scallions, cucumber batons, and hoisin sauce
- Chilled sesame noodles
- Peanut sauce

Pasta Station

Accompanied by garlic bread

- Ciliegine mozzarella with sun-dried tomatoes and basil
- Tricolor lobster ravioli with saffron cream sauce
- Penne with fresh tomato, basil, and shaved Parmesan
- Rigatoni with sweet sausage, spinach, and ricotta
- Farfalle with smoked chicken in parsley pesto sauce
- Mushroom tortellini with four cheese sauce

Satay Station

- Chicken satay
- Sweet chili sauce
- Beef satay
- Spicy peanut sauce
- Vegetable satay
- Green curry sauce

"Taste of Tokyo" Station

- Assorted maki and tekka maki rolls
- Pickled ginger, wasabi, and soy dipping sauces
- Japanese braised short ribs
- Chilled soba noodle salad
- Assorted pickled seaweed

Caviar Station

- North American sturgeon
- Buckwheat blini, chopped egg, chopped red onion
- Capers, parsley, and crème fraîche

Atlantic Ocean Station

- Poached jumbo shrimp with house cocktail sauce
- Stone crab claws (seasonal) with Chesapeake remoulade sauce
- Lobster salad
- Crayfish with drawn butter
- Shucked clams and mussels
- Shucked oysters (market driven)

Sushi Bar

*Note: each sushi station may require two attendants for a per-chef fee.

- An assortment of maki, sushi, and special combo rolls
- Served with wasabi, pickled ginger, and soy dipping sauces

660.
Choose your first courses according to the season. Here are some ideas for great spring and summer foods:

Spring and Summer First Courses

- Baby greens with panko-crusted goat cheese
- Roasted baby beets
- Citrus vinaigrette

✳ ✳ ✳

- Beefsteak tomato napoleon
- Grilled balsamic red onions
- Fresh mozzarella, basil, and extra virgin olive oil

✳ ✳ ✳

- Chilled jumbo shrimp
- Cucumber salad
- House cocktail sauce

✳ ✳ ✳

- Chicken roulade medallions filled with smoked Gouda and parsley pesto
- Jasmine rice salad
- Smoked tomato aioli

✳ ✳ ✳

- Eggless Caesar salad
- Shredded herb chicken
- Shaved Parmesan and garlic croutons

✳ ✳ ✳

Spring and Summer Soups
- Poblano corn chowder
- Jonah crab salad
- Scallion purée

✳ ✳ ✳

- Chickpea soup
- Cantaloupe and honeydew soup
- Lychee nuts
- Mint oil

＊

- Shrimp and carrot soup
- Crab dumplings
- Cinnamon foam

661. Here are some ideas for fall and winter starters:

Fall and Winter First Courses

- Asparagus wrapped in smoked salmon
- Roasted red pepper coulis
- Chervil crème fraîche
- Roasted prawns
- Braised fennel and calypso beans
- Sweet garlic and carrot sauce

＊

- Maryland crab cake
- Minced vegetable tartar sauce
- Organic baby greens

＊

- Endive, apple, and walnut salad
- Crumbled Roquefort cheese
- Aged sherry vinaigrette

＊

- Mesclun greens
- Shaved prosciutto and Parmesan
- Balsamic vinaigrette

Fall and Winter Soups
- Cream of potato soup
- Leek purée
- Cheddar cheese croutons

* * *

- Chestnut soup
- White truffle oil

* * *

- Sweet potato soup
- Candied red peppers
- Basil-scented crème fraîche

* * *

- Pasta and bean soup
- Pancetta crisps
- Shaved Parmesan

* * *

662. For spring and summer, your menu can reflect the kinds of foods that are most appropriate and enjoyable for the season.

Spring and Summer Main Courses
- Soy-glazed grilled salmon
- Shiitake mushrooms and baby bok choy
- Carrot-ginger sauce

* * *

- Spice-crusted red snapper
- Moroccan couscous
- Raspberry-pickled red onions
- Harissa vinaigrette

* * *

- Citrus-glazed arctic char
- Warm fennel and chickpea salad
- Macadamia nut vinaigrette
- Port wine reduction

* * *

- Roasted French-cut breast of chicken
- Braised red cabbage with currants
- Herb spaetzle
- Beet demi-glace

* * *

- Pan-seared duck breast
- Sautéed baby bok choy
- Dried cherry waffle
- Orange-ginger sauce

* * *

- Pan-seared beef tenderloin
- Sautéed spinach and corn fritters
- Bordelaise sauce

663.

Your winter main courses can also reflect the foods of the season. Here are some ideas for fall and winter weddings.

Fall and Winter Main Courses

- BBQ-lacquered salmon
- Edamame, calypso beans, and haricot verts
- Warm blood-orange vinaigrette

✳ ✳ ✳

- Pan-seared sea bass
- Grilled Japanese eggplant and fingerling potatoes
- Wild mushroom ragout

✳ ✳ ✳

- Roasted French-cut breast of chicken au jus
- Roasted beets and chive whipped potatoes

✳ ✳ ✳

- Herb-crusted, double-cut lamb chop
- White bean stew and garlic confit
- Dijon mustard sauce

✳ ✳ ✳

- Porcini-crusted beef tenderloin
- Truffle cream spinach and manchego potato gratin
- Beet demi-glace

• Delmonico steak
• Steamed haricot verts bundles and fried potatoes
• Veal demi-glace

664. In between courses, you might wish to offer a "palate cleanser," a dish of sorbet served in a lovely crystal bowl or even a martini glass. This course traditionally is meant to clear the guests' palates to prepare for the next course. Lemon sorbet is the norm, but you can go with orange, lime, or a mixture of two flavors.

Something to Drink

665. In most standard wedding packages, the price includes a five-hour open bar, usually with top-brand liquors within the stock. Negotiate with your reception hall manager, or deal with a liquor supplier if you're not going through an established wedding hall, to include some great liquors and drinks.

666. Include a wonderful range of top-rated wines as well. Go to www.winespectator.com to read up on the award-winning vintages in all varieties, including the best labels in lower price ranges.

Pairing Up Your Wine

667. Work with a wine expert to match the right wines to your choice of dishes. Again, go to www.winespectator.com for their terrific primer on which wines go with which types of foods. As a brief example—there's much more online, so check it out—here are some of the hottest food-wine pairings to ask about:

• Asian Cuisine and Riesling
• Chicken and Pinot Grigio
• Beef and Cabernet Sauvignon
• Pork and Syrah
• Lamb and Zinfandel
• Veal and Pinot Noir

For wine and cheese pairings, such as for your cocktail hour, here are the matching formulas used by caterers and entertaining experts:

• Strong-tasting cheeses like cheddar go best with Syrah
• Older cheeses like Gruyere go best with Chardonnay
• Younger, more acidic cheeses like goat cheese go best with a highly acidic wine like Sauvignon Blanc
• Salty cheeses like Roquefort go best with sweet dessert wines like Sauterne
• Creamy cheeses like Brie go best with heavier red wines like Cabernet
• Herb cheeses go best with richer, earthier red wines with lots of body

668. Before the wedding, have a wine tasting with your family or bridal party, so that you can taste and rate your favorite vintages. Take notes; these wines may become your long-lasting favorites.

669. Go for signature drinks. If you wish to limit your bar supply, ask the bar manager to create a menu including only certain types of drinks available at the bar. For example, martinis, cosmopolitans, vodka tonics, gin and tonics, and other traditional drinks can be printed on several visible menu cards at the bar so guests know not to order Long Island iced teas.

670. Go for cultural drinks, like mojitos, which are very hot right now. Check out www.foodtv.com for great, ethnically motivated, and multicultural drink ideas as a way to fill your drink menu with the hottest tastes from around the world.

671. Go for fun drinks that match the theme and style of your wedding. For instance, at a beach wedding, you can go for brightly colored mixed drinks and frozen daiquiris. At a winter wedding, you can go with spiked hot cider as one option.

672. Invest some thought into after-dinner drinks, like cappuccino and espresso, crowd favorites, as well as Irish coffees and Jamaican coffees for those who appreciate a great twist on their usual after-dinner coffee.

673. Stock some terrific liqueurs for after-dinner drinks. Talk to your bar manager about the many creative options for Grand Marnier, Cognac, brandy, and the like.

674. At an informal wedding, make up a bar menu where you've given creative, personalized names to all the drinks. Name the espresso with Sambuca after your dad if it's his favorite post-dinner drink. Name a margarita after your friend (e.g., "Mandy's High Society Margarita"). Go with wedding-themed drinks, like a White Russian you've renamed "Bridal Bliss" just for your event. Have some fun with the names! It adds a bit of personality to your drink menu.

675. Look into the best wines from around the world. Give your wedding a global air with vintages that you've selected from the following recently named wine hot zones: Italy, New York State, Washington State, Spain, Argentina, and especially South Africa, where wineries are springing up with the raves of wine connoisseurs.

676. And then, of course, there's champagne. The most important thing is to make it *good* champagne, not a brand bought because it's cheap. Invest well in this— it's your wedding day. Look up champagne reviews, again, at www.winespectator.com and choose the finest—even if it's just a one-fill for each guest.

677. Stock champagne at your open bar for a truly elegant wedding.

678. A wonderful new way that champagne is being served at weddings is with *garnish*. Bartenders are dropping into each champagne flute a single, perfect strawberry, or a few raspberries, a slice of star fruit, or a few ripe pomegranate seeds.

679. Mix in a small amount of fruit juice, like mango, pomegranate, raspberry, cherry, apricot, pink grapefruit, orange, or any other tasty juice that gives champagne some color and a complementary taste. Choose the fruit add-in or fruit juice that will make the newly hued champagne match the color scheme of your wedding.

680. Look for special dessert wines: separate vintages that are specifically matched and most complementary to your dessert menu. Check out www.winespectator.com to get the lowdown on the latest, best-rated dessert wines. Be sure to look into something called Australian "stickies," which—despite the name—are actually a class of wonderful sweet dessert wines that are all the rage among party caterers and brides and grooms alike. Check it out, and have a taste. This could be the perfect wine for your cake cutting and the closing hours of your reception, when the regular wines just don't work with the sweets you're serving.

681. Be sure to provide plenty of attractive nonalcoholic beverages for kids and for adults who don't wish to partake of any alcohol. From soft drinks to lemonade, iced tea or fruit-infused iced tea to punches with a little bit of carbonation, your soft-drink menu can be just as enticing as your bar menu.

682. At warm-weather weddings, especially outdoor and beach weddings, have servers offer guests plenty of ice water, dressed up with lemon or lime slices.

683. At winter weddings, go with comfort drinks that remind you all of warm childhood memories: hot chocolate with plenty of marshmallows or whipped cream is ideal, and guests *love* such treats at wedding wind-downs!

chapter 19

Just Desserts

Then, of course, there's that cake! That beautiful, tiered wedding cake you've been dreaming about…

Cake Design

684. Go with a traditional, all-white bridal cake, tiered and frothy with icing.

685. Do as so many brides and grooms are doing these days, and choose a cake that's a little less traditional but still absolutely gorgeous. Instead of circular tiers, go for tiers of a different shape. Couples today are choosing ovals, squares, rectangles, or they're going geometric with cakes designed to look like a pyramid.

686. A hugely growing trend right now is to forget about the one giant wedding cake in the corner of the room; that five-tiered masterpiece that tempts guests who go over to "visit" it and await its serving. Now, the trend is to have individual, smaller wedding cakes, rather than the big one. You can do as many couples have done by centering each guest table with a beautifully sculpted and frosted wedding cake that's a smaller rendition, tiered and iced, decorated masterfully with iced designs, flowers, and touches of color. Each table of guests gets to dig into their own cake right after you and your groom cut into your own slightly larger version on your main table.

687. Special wedding cakes right now are *chocolate*, as opposed to those all-white bridal cakes with white cake inside and strawberry filling. Even the icing is a rich buttercream chocolate, topped with chocolate roses and chocolate shavings. Love the idea of chocolate but still can't commit to the idea of a brown-colored cake? Go with white chocolate instead.

688. Another hot trend in wedding cakes today, giving them a decidedly non-bridal look, is to select a cake that, with the help of a talented cake artisan, looks like something else. By that, I mean a wedding cake that looks like a big wrapped gift box complete with a ribbon made from fondant. Or a cake that's designed to look like a glass slipper, a flower-strewn carriage, or—one of my favorites—a topiary. Imagine this: an actual floral topiary inserted into a large, square cake that's been frosted and piped to look like a topiary planter, iced in delicate designs on the sides. This surprising touch thrills guests who will marvel at your creativity, and at your cake baker's delicious dessert.

689. Decorate your cake with color instead of all- white icing and piping designs. Now, especially if your gown will be decorated with color, so too can your cake with an all-white frosting or fondant. Use pink, lilac, red, or your choice of color designs piped onto the cake, plus roses and borders as you wish.

690. Decorate your cake with fresh flowers cascading from top tier to bottom. With the help of a floral designer, you can choose a lovely stream of unique blooms plus greenery that will make your cake look incredible.

691. Have the cake artist copy the lace design on your gown to bring out the beautiful style you've chosen to wear and make it match your very symbolic wedding cake.

692. Choose the number of tiers that you and your groom have been together—if it's a manageable one to five years, that is. Couples who have been together for more than ten years should skip this idea. It's just dangerous then.

693. Have your initials monogrammed in frosting or chocolate powder on the cake.

694. Borrow from cake designers and do your initials on the cake in edible gold leaf. In some cultures, this edible gold leaf is symbolic of great riches and prosperity. They work it into many angles of wedding receptions, from garnishing the food to putting accents on other desserts. Check with a cake baker or gourmet specialty food store to inquire more about edible gold leaf for cakes.

695. Look at cake designers' work in sugar-paste molded flowers that look like the real thing. You'll be amazed at the attention to detail, in how real those roses look with the curls of their petals, the amazingly lifelike lily of the valley, even the clear dewdrops that have been painted onto these works of art. Similarly, look at marzipan flowers and greenery or marzipan fruits with greenery for a natural-bounty look.

696. Top your cake with a porcelain cascade of flowers that you will then take home after the wedding and display in your home. This floral artistry in a flexible drape or a circular wreath often finds a place of honor where you'll display your wedding photo—in a glass case or hanging on the wall as part of a display.

697. Top your cake with figurines that mean a lot to you. Perhaps your groom gave you a Lladro figurine for your first holiday together: look at the bridal figurines in that design and have your cake artist expertly attach it and secure it to your cake. As a note of warning, be sure to weigh any figurines or heavier crystal objects that you plan to display on your cake. Your cake baker needs to know how much weight the top layers of cake will have to support so that he or she can design functional and secure tier-separators, or place a sturdier support under the top tier. Failing to take this precautionary step can give you a very unspecial moment when your heavy figurine alters the balance of the cake, causing it all to come crashing to the ground.

698. A new look that's growing in cake toppers is placing a tiara on the cake and surrounding it with a draping of fresh flowers to match your own bouquet. It sounds strange on paper, but once you see the glittering effect, it's wonderful.

699. Use the pearl work of your gown and perhaps your jewelry and carry that theme to your cake décor. Cake designer experts can pipe on simulated pearls made of icing for a marvelously pearl-studded look to your cake.

700. Add some color to your cake's layers by attaching a length of ribbon in your wedding colors around the bottom half of each layer. Secure in front with a sprig of tiny flowers and greenery.

Less Formal Weddings

701. Top your cake with something fun, such as those pinwheels you're giving out to guests as a favor.

702. Use children's dolls dressed up as the bride and groom.

703. Dress up dolls in bathing suits and bright shorts for a beach wedding. Add tiny beach balls and other doll accessories to the cake for a playful, whimsical look.

704. Decorate a cake for a beach wedding with seashells and starfish, all washed well and expertly placed, of course.

705. Design your cake to look like a sand-castle, as many cake bakers and experts can do by frosting the cake in castle form and then sprinkling crushed graham crackers all over it to look like "sand."

706. Do one sheet cake in the shape of your initials. It takes some skill with carving out the shape, and icing it, but it's a wonderful, unique effect.

707. Skip the big wedding cake and set out frosted cupcakes in tiers to resemble the *shape* of a wedding cake. It's an adorable, informal look that—when cupcakes are frosted beautifully and topped with tiny piped roses—is a memorable crowd-pleaser.

708. The same concept works with bakery-bought petit fours, frosted miniature cakes that come in a range of pastel colors or whites. Line these pretty cakes up in a wedding cake-like, tiered design on pedestals, and it works beautifully.

Fillings and Flavors

709. According to celebrity wedding cake designer Ron Ben-Israel of Ron Ben-Israel Cakes in New York City, wedding couples are looking for their cakes to remind them of their favorite childhood treats. Again, we're going back to the blissful younger days with cake fillings and flavors that taste like a Mounds Bar with chocolate and coconut.

710. Try a s'mores cake with chocolate, marshmallow, and graham cracker crumbs mixed into a chocolate buttercream frosting.

711. Also special to many couples is a cake modeled after their favorite comfort food: ice cream. Check out the Ben and Jerry's flavors in your supermarket to see if you'd like a mint chocolate chip cake with chocolate cake and minty buttercream frosting.

712. Create a banana, nut, and chocolate cake inspired by Chunky Monkey.

713. A coffee, nut, and vanilla cake would be a delicious treat.

714. Have your baker create a cake with white and dark chocolate chunks mixed in, with a smooth vanilla or chocolate cream filling.

Delicious Wedding Cakes

715. With thanks once again to the catering team at the Westminster Hotel, who provided the menus in the previous chapter, here's a look at some ideas for wedding cake selections.

Westminster Hotel Wedding Cakes

The following are different varieties of wedding cakes and fillings. Please select one cake and one filling.

Cakes	Fillings
Devil's Food	Citrus Mousse
Spiced Vanilla Sponge	Dark Framboise Chocolate Ganache
Banana	Espresso Mascarpone
Carrot	Chocolate Hazelnut Mousse
Yellow Genoise	Banana Pastry Cream
Cocoa Sponge	Nougatine
Almond	Macadamia
Chocolate Soufflé	Peanut Butter Mousse
Coconut	Double Chocolate Pudding
Espresso	Malt Chocolate Ganache
Lemon	Lemon-Scented Cream Cheese

716. Don't forget that cake masters can provide *sauces* to accent your cake. Choose from flavors like these:

• Raspberry

• Vanilla

• Chocolate

• Caramel

• Passion fruit

• Espresso

• Lemon

• Rum

Desserts beyond the Cake

717. The groom's cake is making a comeback as the secondary cake choice to the more traditional wedding cake. Here is where you get to have some fun with fillings and flavors, perhaps going for a liqueur-flavored cake.

718. Design the cake to reflect an interest of the groom's. If he's a soccer player or fan, have the cake designed in the shape of a soccer ball.

719. The football fan gets a cake shaped like a football.

720. The golf fan gets a cake shaped like a golf bag and clubs, or the eighteenth hole, with a sand trap and water hazard.

721. A runner can get a cake designed like a running shoe.

722. You can also go with your groom's occupation, such as a doctor's bag if he's an MD.

723. A "techie" gets a computer.

724. A lawyer gets a stack of law books.

725. A mechanic gets a car.

726. The NASCAR fan can get a racecar cake decorated with his favorite driver's colors and number.

727. A football fan can get his cake done in the shape of his favorite team's helmet.

728. Aside from the groom's cake, you can fill up a Viennese dessert table with any number of pies, tarts, mousses, and truffles for a big buffet of sweets.

729. Skip the calorie buffet and just set out silver bowls filled with strawberries with fresh whipped cream on the side.

730. Have the strawberries chocolate-dipped for true indulgence.

731. A variety of chocolate truffles from Godiva (www.godiva.com) or your favorite chocolate store can be set out in crystal bowls or silver serving platters. Choose from rum balls, key lime, white chocolate, raspberry, coconut, pecan caramel, mango, lemon ganache, and other truffle fillings.

732. Go for great theme-based desserts, such as the Godiva chocolate starfish filled with raspberry sauce, as the perfect treat at a beach or sea-themed wedding.

733. You can have almost any custom shape made by chocolatiers, such as stars, hearts, pyramids, high heel shoes, keys, seashells, snowflakes, butterflies, even luxury cars like Porsches and Ferraris. You can also get your monogram added to the chocolates and select your choice of fillings.

734. Dramatic flambées are also a great way to make your dessert hour special. Trained servers can light the flambé burners so that a curl of flame dances up in the air, and then your bananas or strawberries are flambéed for serving. It's a show and a treat.

735. Don't forget dessert fondues, which have come back to life from near obscurity just a few years ago. Set out several fondue pots with melted white and dark chocolate in them, surrounded by pieces of fruit or pound cake, and fondue serving forks for the dipping.

736. Some couples have even done a marshmallow fondue, with pieces of chocolate, banana, berries, and brownie chunks ready for dipping.

737. Of course, you have your favorite desserts on hand: cheesecakes, white chocolate mousses, pecan pies, cannolis—anything the chef can prepare for your dessert hour.

738. Provide desserts the kids will love, such as cupcakes and brownies, or oversized chocolate chip cookies set on plates with a scoop of ice cream.

739. An ice cream sundae bar is a great choice for less formal weddings. Set up the barrels of homemade ice cream, have servers do the major scooping, and then guests get to top their sundaes with chocolate or vanilla sauces, berry sauces, caramel, nuts, sprinkles, whipped cream, and—of course—a cherry on top.

740.
For sit-down dessert ideas, here once again is the serving desserts menu from the Westminster Hotel.

- Vanilla panna cotta
- Strawberry consommé and balsamic reduction

✳ ✳ ✳

- Orange blossom rice pudding
- Mixed fresh red fruits

✳ ✳ ✳

- Almond and coconut cake
- Lemon cream, Italian meringue, and strawberry coulis

✳ ✳ ✳

- Chocolate hazelnut crunch dome
- Layers of hazelnut crunch and espresso crème brûlée

✳ ✳ ✳

- Dark chocolate and raspberry dome
- Layers of dark chocolate cake and raspberry confit
- Raspberry coulis

✳ ✳ ✳

- Warm fondant chocolate cake with pistachio ice cream
- Banana pecan gratin on a honey chiboust
- Caramel ice cream

***

- Warm apple tart
- Caramel sauce and cinnamon ice cream

***

- Melon consommé with beaume de venise
- Lychee and mango sorbet

***

- Chocolate rice krispie
- Salted peanut butter ice cream

***

- Tarte tatin
- Maple syrup ice cream

chapter 20

Give Your Guests a Show

Your reception will be more than just a lovely dinner, but rather an *experience*, if you give some thought to the more special arrangements you can make for the entertainment. Of course, you're thinking about bands vs. DJs right now, but there are so many more amazing performers you can hire for just a short portion of your cocktail hour, reception dinner, even your after-party. Even your ceremony music can come from one of these options, for something extra-special in the earlier part of your day. Read on to discover truly unique and special ideas to give your guests a real show at your celebration.

Traditional Choices: Bands and DJs

741. Of course, we'll start with the usuals: your choice between hiring a band or hiring a DJ. Many couples find it traditional and part of their wedding dream to have a live band playing at their wedding. If this is you, then spend a lot of time asking friends for referrals to the great bands who played at their weddings, visit band showcases, and audition bands to see and hear how they perform live.

742. If at all possible, try to catch the band you're interested in as they perform at another live event. See how they command the stage and interact with the crowd. It's the best way to really see your band at work.

743. Think about the kinds of songs you want played at your wedding (e.g., more jazz than Top 40 music), and select your potential bands according to their specialty in the kind of music you want.

744. For DJs, try to see the DJ in action with an actual crowd at an actual event. Watch out for way-too-enthusiastic DJs who seem to be annoying the guests or playing music that doesn't fit the crowd.

745. Ask about what any entertainer, band, or DJ will be wearing at the wedding. Preventing those 1970s purple tuxes is one thing, but making sure the female lead singer isn't dressed like a porn star is another. You have a right to ask your entertainers what they plan to wear, and make specific requests that they dress to fit in with the formality of your event. Trust me, you don't want a sex-kitten vamp on stage at your elegant, formal wedding.

746. Know that you can hire a team of DJs, perhaps two CD-spinners who interact with one another, make great banter, and engage your crowd well. Plus, while one's on his break, the other can keep the music going.

747. Get the best of both worlds. The wedding music entertainment industry has been listening to brides and grooms for years. They know the struggle couples face when trying to decide between a band and a DJ, their wish to have a live performance, and budget troubles that might have a couple choosing a DJ over the pricier band they really wanted and thus sacrificing those live songs. They've come up with a solution. Now, you can hire a DJ *and* have a singer or a duo with a guitarist or keyboardist on hand for a short portion of your reception. This interlude from the DJ's spinning is just what you always dreamed of, so ask about combo packages where you get both options. Your guests will love the surprise performance.

Going Outside the Music "Box"

748. Look at bands that aren't necessarily standard wedding bands, such as jazz trios.

749. A classical orchestra will add a touch of elegance to the room.

750. Bands that specialize in Motown music will fill the dance floor all night long, with everyone singing along to their favorite songs (and reliving the memories they bring!).

751. Big Band or swing orchestras (Glenn Miller-style or 1940s-era music) please your entire crowd. Older guests will be thrilled to dance to songs they recognize, and the younger set has its own favorite songs from trendy swing dancing nights at their favorite clubs.

752. Brass bands will ignite the party with their amazing sound, especially when the musicians are real show-men. At some parties, trumpet players put on a real spectacular, throwing their horns up into the air, displaying amazing talent with spotlight solos, and blasting out unique versions of popular music with a twist.

753. Hiring cultural musicians for the cocktail party or for a portion of the reception is very hot right now, and is adding something very special to weddings with a cultural or ethnic flair. Remember, you can break your reception up into portions with different entertainment at each stage or location! Check with international associations for resources to find Japanese wind musicians, Indian bands, Asian dulcimer musicians, or Celtic harpists, flutists, and the like.

754. Look at classical ensembles. As an example of the kinds of musicians you can hire for your cocktail hour or reception (or even your ceremony), here is a sample list of ensembles from the professional musical entertainment company Music in the Air (www.musicintheair.com) in New York City.

Ensembles Available for Performances

- *Two For Tea* – flute and cello or cello and harp or any two instruments
- *The Seville Trio* – flute, violin, and cello or any three instruments
- *White Tie & Tails* – piano, flute, and cello
- *The Embassy Quartet* – two violins, viola, and cello
- *The Heights Quartet* – flute, violin, viola, and cello
- *Brassworks* – trumpets, trombones, and French horn
- *Or any solo or combination of instruments*

755. Of course, for your cocktail hour or the dinner hour of your reception, you can hire supremely romantic strolling violinists.

756. Hire a cellist to play under spotlight as your guests dine.

757. A jazz or opera singer can perform solo as your guests enjoy their meals.

Choosing the Music

758. Always make a play list for your musical entertainers. List your favorite songs, including that for your first dance and all of your special dances of the evening.

759. Similarly, make a "do not play" list of songs you don't want to hear (as well as line dances you hate), to make sure a song that brings back bad memories for anyone is not a part of your day.

Know Your Crowd

760. If you know there will be a large number of older relatives at the party, then advise your entertainer to keep the Top 40 music to the very end of the reception when the "younger people" are up on the dance floor. For the earliest hours of your event, have the entertainer play songs your more senior guests will love and dance to, like Glenn Miller songs, Motown, even music from the 60s. Focus on your crowd and pick songs they'll fully enjoy.

761. Of course, the song you pick for your song will become a lasting memory. It will take you back to your wedding day every time you hear it in the future. So choose well from the songs that are most special to you.

762. If there's a story that goes with your chosen first dance song, such as "This is the song that we danced to together on our first date. When I took his hand, I kind of jumped back after feeling a rush of attraction to him," share that story with all of your wedding guests. Everyone always likes to know the significance of your first dance choice.

763. For special dances, such as the father-daughter dance, check out traditional and nontraditional songs for that tribute twirl. DJs tell me that Luther Vandross's "Dance With My Father Again" is topping the list right now. You can always go with Frank Sinatra classics that are special to your family or your dad's favorite song.

764. No one ever said the special dances with mothers, fathers, and other special people have to be solo, spotlit, slow dances. Shake it up a little and do some swing dancing instead.

765. At one wedding I attended, the bride and her father showed their shared love of celebration by starting off with a very sappy slow dance to a very sappy song that was not their style at all, leading their guests to look at one another questioning, "Are they kidding?" Then the music changed abruptly to something that was more *them*. That's when the father started pulling people up out of their chairs to do a conga line behind him and his daughter. To this bride and her dad, sharing the moment with their guests and poking fun at the sentimental, sappy first dance was so *them!*

766. Let your music do the talking as you play songs for your parents, grandparents, and your new in-laws.

767. Don't forget your friends! It makes the wedding so special for them when you all are out there dancing to "your song," just like you always have for the years of your friendship.

768. At one wedding, the bride and groom played a little trick on their close band of friends by having the DJ publicly play a taped recording of all the friends singing "Sledgehammer" by Peter Gabriel, which someone had audiotaped during the group's pub-crawl wind-down one evening years ago. From the first notes of the song, all of the friends knew exactly what it was, and it was the highlight of the night when they all started singing it together again in the center of the dance floor. Every tone-deaf note was hysterical, and it brought back one of their best-shared memories.

769. For you both, the most special songs of the evening might be traditional songs from your heritage. You don't have to hire a polka band, but rather ask your DJ to play a traditional song from your background.

770.

Jewish music includes "Hatikvah," "Hava Nagilah," "Jerusalem the Golden," "Mein Yiddishe Miedele," "Yiddishe Momme." Play popular Jewish holiday songs such as "Dayenu," "Eyn Keloheynu," "O Hanukah," "My Dreidel," "Hag Purim," and "Baruch Eloheynu," if your wedding will take place during or near holiday times of the year.

771.

Irish songs include "Danny Boy," "Peg O' My Heart," "Believe Me If All Those Endearing Young Charms," "The Irish Jubilee," "Jolly Irishman," "Let Me Call You Sweetheart," "Londonderry Air," "My Wild Irish Rose," "The Rose of Tralee," "Sweet Rosie O'Grady," "Too-Ra-Loo-Ra Loo-Ral," and "When Irish Eyes Are Smiling."

772.

Go global with music from other ethnic backgrounds, whether or not they're your own. Here are some of the most popular ethnic picks from today's weddings—ask your band or DJ for additional choices:

- *Italian*: "Adagio," "Tango Italiano," "Volare," "That's Amore," "Tarantella," "Besame Mucho," "Come On A My House," "O Sole Mio," "Santa Lucia," the theme from "The Godfather"
- *Latin*: "Guantanamera," "Oye Como Va," "Beautiful Maria of My Soul"

- *Brazilian*: "A Felicidad," "O Grande Amor," "Girl From Ipanema," "One Note Samba"
- *Polish*: "Beer Barrel Polka," "Polish Wedding March"
- *Island/Reggae*: "Jump In the Line," "The Lion Sleeps Tonight," "Many Rivers to Cross," "Red, Red Wine," "Jammin'," "I Got You Babe (the UB40 version)," "No Woman, No Cry"

773. Check music suppliers and international associations to see if you can get compilation CDs of your favorite ethnic songs performed by international artists.

774. Look for CDs of harp music, flute music, soft jazz, and piano music to play during your cocktail hour *instead* of hiring a live musician. Set up a multiple-disc player in the corner, load your chosen instrumental CDs and make lovely ambience for about $20, as opposed to $200 for hiring professionals.

775. For a beach-themed wedding, one couple bought steel drum music CDs to play at their non-island wedding, and it gave them a great mood setter for their party.

776. Of course, at your more informal reception or after-party, there's always the option of karaoke, which is a ton of fun if your crowd regularly goes out to sing at a bar for karaoke night and everyone already has their own "specialty songs." You can rent a karaoke machine, buy one for future parties, or even hire a karaoke DJ with a full set of equipment to work your party. Just imagine all your groomsmen with their ties off, shirts opened at the collar, slightly red-eyed and swaying off-beat as they belt out "Summer Wind" or your mothers joining the bridesmaids to sing the ever-cheesy "It's Raining Men." This is what memories are made of, and it can make your group experience that much more special for all of you.

Dinner and a Show

777. The new trend in receptions is giving guests a *show*. Not just Uncle Harold shimmying in way-too-tight pants on the dance floor, although that is a show in itself. We're talking about entertainers brought in to make your reception something completely different from any other wedding your guests have been to before. At one Moroccan-inspired wedding, the bride and groom hired three belly dancers to work their crowd during the cocktail hour.

778. At an Irish wedding, the couple hired—for just a small donation to the team's travel fund for competitions—a troupe of adorable Irish ceili dancers, little girls in their embroidered dresses with their hair in ringlets, to perform three numbers at the opening of the reception.

779. At an outdoor wedding on the lawn of a grand estate, the couple actually hired several ballet dancers from a local ballet school to do a *pas de deux* before the ceremony started. This show started off the day perfectly fitting the bride's wish for a magical-princess wedding that was, according to her, "like a scene from a snowglobe." The guests were captivated and enthralled by the performance.

780. At a Latin-inspired wedding, the couple hired three teams of professional salsa dancers to inspire their crowd to get out on the dance floor. Later in the evening, the professional dancers judged a salsa dance competition among the guests, some of whom really hit it off during the contest!

781. At a beach wedding, the couple hired hula dancers from a local dance school to perform several traditional dances, including ancient Hawaiian wedding performances.

782. Hiring entertainers doesn't have to be for a cultural or upscale wedding. At informal outdoor family-style weddings, couples have hired jugglers, face painters, acrobats, and other artists who made the reception a hit among guests young and old.

For real, over-the-top entertainment hired to make your wedding extra special, likening it to a big time event like an Academy Awards party, consider the following artists-for-hire.

783. Trumpeters can announce your entrance.

784. Bagpipers can open and close your ceremony, and even lead a walking procession to the nearby ceremony.

785. Gospel choirs can belt out inspirational music that will get your guests clapping along.

786. Caricaturists can draw a likeness of your guests.

787. Magicians and illusionists can entertain both children and adults.

788. Holiday carolers are perfect for your winter holiday wedding. Professional singing groups can dress up in Victorian-era outfits with winter muffs and top hats to sing Christmas carols.

789. Ice sculptors on site will create masterpieces right outside your reception hall windows.

790. A cappella singing groups will entertain your crowd or single out guests to serenade.

791. Acrobats and aerialists for an outdoor or circus-themed wedding will delight guests young and old with a breathtaking show of daring and strength.

792. Broadway performances, such as a trio of Broadway singers, can come to perform Broadway standards for your crowd. A big hit at a recent wedding was the two Broadway starlets who showed up to sing a few numbers from the movie and musical *Chicago*, the couple's favorite show. It brought down the house!

793. A growing favorite, most likely inspired by Elton John and Billy Joel, is to have dueling piano players who compete against one another in an amazingly expert performance for your crowd's vote of applause.

794. Hire renaissance performers for your renaissance-themed wedding.

795. Hire a Las Vegas-style lounge act (cleaned up for family viewing).

Don't Forget the Kids

At weddings where a large group of kids will attend, such as at an outdoor family-style wedding, a beach or backyard wedding, or even a formal wedding where kids have been taken someplace less formal for their entertainment, look at these entertainment ideas:

796. Balloon artists

797. Temporary tattoo application

798. Pony rides

799. Experts running inflatable games like moonwalks, sumo suits, and Velcro walls

800. Laser tag games

801. Karaoke for kids (in a separate location)

802. Costumed characters or holiday characters like Santa Claus or the Easter Bunny, even the Tooth Fairy, to show up for a surprise visit that thrills little kids

803. Storytellers

804. Hayrides out into a nearby pumpkin patch or farm with a corn maze, where they will be entertained and even pick their own small pumpkins for an autumn wedding treat

Roll the Videotape!

805. Some best men are way too nervous to give their toast in front of a crowd. So, through the magic of videotape and the help of a video-editor friend, they're creating toast *videos* complete with soundtracks and photos of the couple, pictures of the best man with the groom, and the relief of not having to face those nerves on the wedding day.

806. Couples are also creating videotaped presentations to open their receptions. With the help of a videographer and editor, they're playing on plasma screen televisions or large screens a welcome message from the two of them, along with photo montages of them as a couple.

807. Some couples even include videotaped footage of the moment when the groom proposed to the bride. Showing all of the wedding guests this footage of "the moment it all began" is the perfect way to start off the celebration of "the moment right now."

808. Of course, this videotaped presentation about the bride and groom can be a surprise *for* the bride and groom, created as a gift by a filmmaker friend or anyone who knows how to use their own handheld camcorder and home computer's video editing system.

809. As a gift to the bride and groom, the camcorder-toting friend can interview their family members and friends—as recently as at the rehearsal dinner—and portray those loved ones' wishes for the couple, favorite memories, and best advice about how to have a happy marriage.

810. Children of the couple can be the stars of a special video presentation, talking about how happy they are to have their new stepmommy or new stepdaddy, even singing a song or just blowing kisses into the camera for the happy couple.

811. And, of course, just like at the Academy Awards or Golden Globes, a touching video tribute to a departed parent or sibling can include that much-missed relative in the big day, sharing footage of them in their best and happiest times with the bride and groom as a priceless gift to all guests.

chapter 21

The After-Party

Instead of closing down your reception at 10 or 11 PM when your booking time for the room expires, why not follow the trend of moving to another location for an after-party? Keep the celebration going with your smaller, more select group of friends and family in the following ways.

812. Forget about taking off for alone time, just the two of you. Today's brides and grooms are fine with staying longer with their guests—many of whom they haven't seen for months or years before their wedding day—in a more casual setting where they can sit and talk without the chaos and constant greetings of the large crowd, cake-cutting time, and other demands at the reception. You and your groom have the honeymoon to be alone together. Spend time with your loved ones for just a few hours more after your reception.

Extending Invitations to the After-Party

813. Invite just your immediate family, closest relatives, the bridal party, and your best friends to the after-party, giving them prior notice before the big night so that they can plan to attend. It would be a shame for your best friends to have to leave when the babysitter back home is expecting their return. Send a separate invitation for this get-together, or enclose a separate card in each invited guest's formal invitations packet.

814. Send these guests an invitation via email. The website www.evite.com has some cute email invitation designs, and your "inner circle" can also see by the recorded responses who else is coming to the after-party.

815. It might be wise to let your invited guests know that this party is *exclusive*. Since other guests might get offended at being left off the list for this gathering, you might wish to subtly let your invited guests know that they should remain hush-hush. No party crashers welcome, except for your own last-second invitation extensions.

After-Party Locations

816. A change in venue is the best idea possible to set a new mood for the after-party. The most popular trend right now is going to a separate lounge, a dimly lit, more intimate atmosphere, perhaps in a private room or just a corner table where you can all enjoy the scene.

817. A romantic jazz club could be the perfect destination for your after-party—great music, great atmosphere, and quiet jazz for that wind-down time.

818. Head to a cigar bar, especially one that has a private party room with leather couches and an entertainment system with great sound.

819. For a more informal gathering, head to a sports bar for a few pitchers of beer, shoot a game of pool, play darts, and have some fun with guests who wouldn't normally be out at a sports bar lifting beer mugs to your happiness. One bride told me, "It was so much fun to have our parents out in our regular Saturday night hang-out place. They got to share a little of our lifestyle, and we had a *blast* seeing them interact with our friends and our favorite bartender. This made for a great memory."

820. Take the after-party to a restaurant with a great view, perhaps a large table on an outdoor terrace overlooking the beach. If you weren't able to have a beach wedding for some reason, this after-party would fulfill your wishes for that oceanside gathering.

821. Take the party to the honeymoon suite or a penthouse in the hotel where you're staying. Some suites are just gorgeous with great views, and they give an elegant, indulgent feel to your party.

822. Take the party home to your place, or to your parents' place. So many parents of the bride and groom do this anyway, inviting their friends and close relatives over after the wedding that it's just natural for you and your friends to do the same. An at-home after-party can be the most relaxing thing after your busy day, and it allows you to once again share a special family time in the home where you've had so many other special family times.

After-Party Styles

823. Cocktails and coffee are the usual order for an after-party, with espresso and cappuccino on the menu, along with after-dinner drinks.

824. For the couple who loves being young at heart, a pizza party could be just the late-night style in demand.

825. Caterers tell me that for the new after-party, couples are ordering up a buffet of bar-food hits: buffalo wings, quesadillas, and chips and dip.

826. Late-night partiers are familiar with the "diner run" for food after a long night of bar-hopping. So, receptions that end late can turn the after-party into a diner-esque snack-fest, with breakfast foods such as waffles, pancakes, and omelets, or those artery-clenching French fries with brown gravy and mozzarella. Just don't wear the wedding gown to the diner unless you *really* need to be the center of attention.

827. Then there's always the after-party where it's nothing but coffee and Krispy Kremes, much to guests' delight.

828. Getting away from the fast food, diner food, and childhood pajama party snacks, you can go more upscale with a catered late-night cocktail party. Pass around serving dishes filled with hot *hors d'oeuvres* like crab puffs, endive with cream cheese and caviar, and mini turkey meatballs in a cranberry glaze.

829. Fondue parties are also hot for the post-reception party. Guests who've hit it off during the night can bond over bread cubes and cheese, or go for the chocolate fondue assortment.

830. A wine and cheese party is also a hot idea, with a lineup of great wines from your favorite vintages, and an assortment of hard and soft cheeses, breadsticks, and fruits like grapes and strawberries for a simple, but elegant, spread back at home.

After-Party Activities

831. It might not be where you are or what's on the menu that is the main attraction for your after-party. Since you are finally able to spend some quiet time alone with your closest family and friends, the allure of the after-party is finally getting some time to talk.

832. Now is the time when you, as bride and groom, will be privy to the many stories of your day that you missed out on while you were mingling, out taking pictures, or out of sight before the ceremony started. Now is when you'll find out from your parents about your guests' reactions and comments about the décor at the ceremony site, the adorable way your flower girl skipped down the aisle instead of walking (you missed that while you were out doing deep breathing in the vestibule!), and the details of how your bridesmaid wound up getting the phone number of that very hot bartender. These are the priceless bits of info that are shared with you *right now*, instead of faded from memory or forgotten by the time you come home from your honeymoon!

833. And speaking of not waiting, you won't have to wait to see some pictures from your wedding day. Guests with digital cameras can fire up their machines to show you those amazing candids of you and your groom and scenes you missed from that one rocking guest table in the corner. You can hand the camera around for everyone to see, or use an adapter to display all the pictures on your big-screen TV for a group viewing.

834. The same goes for any video footage your guests took during your day. Just load the tape and play, getting your immediate gratification and a beautiful show of how lovely you looked coming down the aisle. Right now you get to see it, while the moment is still fresh and you're still on your bridal buzz.

835. Couples who love games can fire up the Wedding Mad Libs, or even a trivia contest about the day, written up by you beforehand. Ask questions that are relatively easy ("What was the song we danced to for our first dance?") as well as tougher, more observational ones ("What color robe was the priest wearing?" or "What was the first fast dance the DJ played?"). The winner gets a gift certificate for a romantic dinner for two, and everyone loves the challenge.

836. Get outside and play, especially if it's a snowy winter's night. Go for a long walk through the neighborhood, sledding, or even have a snowball fight. On a summer's night, head outside for a cocktail party by the pool, go for a night swim, hit the hot tub, or play nighttime volleyball.

837. Relax by the fireplace and just hang out with nothing on the agenda. Quiet time to chat might be all you want for this gathering. So get out those great blankets, kick off your shoes, and lounge.

838. Some after-parties are designed to last all night long. With the reception ending in the late-night hours, some couples allow their guests to stay as late as they wish—if they have unlimited use of the reception site, such as at a beach house or their own home. Several brides and grooms have told me that after their receptions, they led a small group of friends out onto the beach, where they all set out blankets, polished off the last of the champagne, and stayed up to view the sunrise. Talk about making the most of the wedding day! There isn't a more romantic way to end the night, or to start your first full day as husband and wife.

Ditching the Crowd

839. After the after-party, or perhaps the very first minute after the reception closes down and you can *finally* be alone with one another, say your good-byes to your guests and take off for your well-earned privacy, just the two of you. It could be ordering up some room service (e.g., champagne, dessert, snacks) and changing into something a little more comfortable, or digging into those great chocolates you gave out as favors at the wedding.

840. Of course, you might not feel the need to run straight back to the honeymoon suite, but rather would like to take a nice long *private* ride in the limousine along the coast, through the park, or even through holiday-decorated neighborhoods or the "rich areas" where the mansions are. Couples tell me that this "riding off into the sunset" cruise in the limo was a very romantic and very transitional time for them.

841. Head out to the beach, just the two of you, to watch the lights of ships passing by in the far distance, and stay there to catch the sunrise in the morning.

842. Go to a park, lay out a blanket, and just relax under the stars. Bonus points for seeing shooting stars to make a wish on.

843. Romantic couples can take a picnic basket and something to toast each other with to a hill overlooking a marina or a beautiful view of the city lights. Okay, so you'll probably be surrounded by teenagers in parked cars with the windows steamed up, but it's romantic nonetheless.

844. If you'd rather not go for a ride, set up the outside balcony of your hotel room with a safe candle, some strawberries to snack on, and your champagne flutes, turn on some lovely music and slow dance in the open air.

845. If the resort where you're marrying has hammocks out on the beach, steal away to "hang out" there.

846. Of course, there's always the option of taking a bubble bath or jumping into your in-room hot tub together, with those champagne glasses in hand and those fluffy, complimentary robes waiting for you afterward.

847. Whatever you're doing and wherever you go, now is the time when you can share with one another all the details of your wedding day. Tell him what you thought when you first saw him while you were walking down the aisle, how you were not nervous at all this morning, or how much you loved the vows he wrote.

848. Better yet, this is when he'll tell *you* what he thought when he first saw you, which are words you'll undoubtedly remember forever.

849. This is the perfect time to start a ritual for your married life together. For instance, if the two of you ordered up a piece of cheesecake right before midnight, then perhaps you can celebrate future anniversaries by having "our piece of cheesecake" on the night of your anniversary for years to come.

850. Finish off the journal of your wedding plans, the diary you've been keeping to record all the details and your thoughts about the upcoming wedding for the past year, with one last entry from the two of you. Then close the book on your single life.

851. Whether you'll enjoy your wedding night at home or in a hotel suite, decorate for the ultimate in romance. Grooms, this one's for you: surprise your bride-to-be by decorating your honeymoon suite ahead of time, filling the room with flowers and candles, and lining up a romantic soundtrack on the CD player. Lay out her satin robe for her, and put that sandalwood massage oil right on the bedside table. Sprinkle rose petals on the carpet leading up to the bed (we love that!), and set out a card that tells her how much you love her. Then get ready to *really* celebrate your new marriage.

PART FIVE:

Additional Details

chapter 22

Impressive Invitations

852. For the complete ins and outs of invitation etiquette, formality rules, and wording templates, visit the big bridal websites or the sites of individual wedding invitation companies. They often offer primers on the correct way to word your invitation according to your own wedding's conditions (such as who is hosting, or if it's a second wedding, etc.).

853. Keep in mind that the rules in invitations have shifted a bit, allowing you *much* more freedom to break from the old "formal weddings *must* have a white or ecru invitation with black print" mandate. Now that the black and white rule is being replaced by significantly more unique and personalized styles in design, you can make your invitations stand out by using colored paper stock and colored print, graphics, even a photo of the two of you.

For the latest and greatest in special new invitation options, I spoke with top specialist Leslie Vismara of Vismara Invitations (www.vismarainvitations.com), who offers the following tips to you.

854. "Wedding invitations are about a celebration, so why not have fun? Show your personalities and who you are as a couple, as well as all the 'when and where' of an invitation. What's most important is that it conveys to your family and friends the happiness and excitement you're feeling over your upcoming event."

855. "Relax in how you word your invitation. Rather than stick strictly to the formats, include a quote that means a lot to you. Yes, an invitation is supposed to convey by its formal wording what guests are to expect of your celebration, but you can do that creatively by adding a line at the bottom that says 'Dinner, drinks, and dancing to follow' or, for an outdoor wedding, 'Leave the stilettos at home.' Such wording allows you to communicate without all the formality, allowing you to sound like *you* in your invitation."

856. "You've put a lot of time and thought into choosing the perfect location for your wedding, so convey the sense of your locale in your invitation. Use a graphic of the beach, the types of trees that grow there, or the types of flowers you're using."

857. "Check out your options in colored paper and ink to convey a sense of place as well. If your wedding will be barefoot on the beach, use a speckly cream paper to resemble sand, along with a sea-blue ink for your wording. If you'll have an Aspen holiday wedding, choose winter-white paper, along with a metallic silver ink."

858. "Go creative with the binding or shape of your invitation. You could do a regular folded invitation, or you could use a collection of single, separate pages tied at the top with a color-coordinated ribbon." Also popular are shaped invitations, and those that are creatively folded like those that arrive as rectangles, but fold out into heart shapes. Big on the market right now are invitations printed on the front of rice paper fans in an Asian style, or folded invitations that slip into rice-paper pockets.

859. "Or create a book program with several pages, bound, including an opening page to announce your upcoming wedding, a page for the ceremony location and time, and a page for the reception location and time along with any special notes like that 'dinner, dancing, and drinks' or a note about wardrobe. The last page might be a fun note from you, like 'We can't wait to share our day with you,' or a photo of the two of you."

860. "If you do a booklet, have some fun with the design of it. Include quotes that are special to you, including any sayings or quotes that are from your heritage or background."

861. "Talk with your invitations designer about including unique elements to your invitations packet, especially if you're having a destination wedding. For a recent destination I worked on, the bride and I envisioned and created an invitations book that opened up with a map of the island of St. John, and then the inside pages included the wedding information."

862. "If you have a wonderful multicultural story between the two of you, or if you encompass that wonderful trend of long-distance romance working out, then you might wish to design a map of the world with stars on 'His' and 'Hers' cities, countries, or even continents, perhaps with a note saying that love crosses all boundaries and barriers, flies great distances, and nothing can prevent a great love from growing."

863. "A great invitations packet can include a page with your picture as a couple, and the brief story of how you met." Remember, some of your more distant guests and longtime family friends might not have had the chance to meet your intended. This invitations packet, then, is a welcome introduction and a heartwarming look at how happy the two of you are. This option makes the new invitation amazingly more special than those traditional black and white invitations from years ago!

864. "Often, invitations are something that brides and grooms tend to look for a little later in their planning process, seeing it as more of a functional item than what it truly is. Your invitation is incredibly special in how it conveys the tone of you and your party to your guests, and—since your invitation is often displayed in your home after the wedding, perhaps with your wedding photo in a frame—it becomes as much of a treasured keepsake as your wedding day photos or videos. So keep that in mind when looking at designs and thinking about how to convey your individual style to your guests. Your invitation should not be an afterthought."

865. "Since so many guests may be coming into your town for the wedding, it's important to think of the needs of your out-of-town guests. In your invitations packet, be sure to provide great directions, even graphically designed maps, and full details on all of the wedding weekend events. You might even add a page to your invitations packet that lists the various activities you have planned, along with contact information for each event's individual host."

866. "Sending a 'Save the Date' card is a very wise idea in our hurried and overscheduled lives. Especially if you're planning a destination wedding, a wedding held on a holiday weekend, or if you have many guests who will need to fly in or travel a great distance to attend, be sure to send a beautiful, well-designed Save the Date card months in advance of sending the actual invitations."

867. "You can make your Save the Date card creative as well, including that story of your relationship, contact information for airlines or hotels, and letting guests know about any group discount rates you might have negotiated with hotels or even with the airline itself. Provide a group discount code on this card, and give your guests a very special break on their travel expenses on your behalf."

868.
Don't forget to print up terrific, graphically beautiful invitations to your other wedding events, such as the rehearsal dinner or bridal brunches. You'll definitely want to design an attractive, theme-appropriate, and fun invitation for each of these events to convey the style of the gathering and also your personalities. You could go with traditional invitations or even printed postcards with a fun picture of the two of you on the front side.

If you'd rather not go through the same design and ordering process that you did with your official wedding invitations, these are the ones you can quite easily create yourselves! While you could go to Office-Max or Staples for designed paper and just print them out on your home computer using standard bridal graphics and colored ink in great fonts, why not go a step further? Now, there's terrific software on the market that can give you so much more creating power and skill.

Check out PrintingPress, the PC-compatible CD-ROM invitation software package from www.mountaincow.com, 800-797-6269. This program offers you an impressive supply of one hundred color graphics, thirty possible invitation design layouts, plus twelve different fonts, allowing you to custom-design your own invitations to your own unique and personalized parties. Better yet, you can use this software again and again in the future, such as when you're inviting everyone to celebrate your first anniversary or even (gulp) a possible baby shower! Check it out!

869. And, of course, for these "lesser" parties and wedding weekend events, there's always www.evite.com and other online invitation services where you can email your friends and family with stylish and convenient invitations.

Programs and Other Printed Items

870. For your wedding programs, make this booklet something extraordinary. Again, choose great papers for your folded, trifold, or booklet formats, use great colored ink and special fonts, include all pertinent information about what's going on in your ceremony, and include a page with the story of your relationship. For an extra-special kick, as well as a treasured keepsake, you might wish to add a page with the story of how your groom proposed to you and include a picture of the two of you from that night.

871. No great wedding program would be complete without a printed thank you to all of the people who helped plan and create your wedding. Include your parents; all of the many helpers you had within your bridal party; friends who volunteered to help make favors or bake for the wedding weekend activities; even your wedding coordinator, who deserves a very public thank you for her months of hard work. Being included in the wedding program is an honor for all involved, making them feel special and very loved and appreciated by you.

872. We've already tackled place cards and menu cards for your guests' tables, but I wanted to encourage you to look into the various design elements for these personal touches at your reception. Check out great paper sources, or commission a calligrapher to handwrite guests' names on their place cards if you'd rather go classic than computer-created. A graphic artist can do amazing things with place card creation, including laser-cut paper, holograms for those silver-and-white-themed weddings, including pictures on place cards—anything you can imagine for this extra-special touch.

chapter 23

Photos and Video

Photography and videography are two areas where brides and grooms often spend a significant chunk of their wedding budget. While, yes, these two services are often surprisingly expensive out there on the wedding market, it's also because your pictures and video are the only truly lasting mementos of your wedding day that you will keep out in your home and enjoy countless times in the future. Wedding photojournalists tell me that when you're looking at it in terms of an *investment* in your family memories and you add up the value of showing these pictures to your kids some day, the actual dollar amount is not much compared to what these images of your day will be worth to you in the future. If you keep in mind that most people say "their wedding pictures" as an answer when asked what one thing they'd run back into their burning home to retrieve, you'll agree that these snapshots and images are worth it.

For many couples who lost a family member shortly after their weddings, whether to illness or accident, having this last footage of their happy, healthy relative dancing and enjoying their family also becomes something truly special to the family as a whole.

So read on to see how you can make your wedding photos and video footage even more special right now, and right on into the future.

Your Wedding Photos

873. Skip the traditional posed pictures where you're all lined up and smiling straight ahead, and instead go for more playful, candid pictures. Talk to your photographer ahead of time about his or her "style" with photos. Some experts consider themselves to be more portrait-oriented, and others call themselves "photojournalists" who are more content with capturing the action as it happens, rather than placing people for stiff reenactments. You'll know when you've found the expert who matches your wished-for style of wedding pictures: their sample books will be filled with just the right mix of planned and spontaneous snapshots that capture not just the look of your day, but the *feel* of your day. There is a difference.

874. Mix up the appearance of the photos you order. By this, I mean getting some pictures in full color, some in black and white (which is a very classic, elegant, and timeless look that is also most flattering to the subjects of the picture). Also, look at the more artistic options of sepia (which looks like an old-fashioned picture in tones of brown and white), as well as hand-painted black and whites (a traditional black and white photograph with some pastel colors adding depth and hue to the images in the pictures). It's a lovely look and one of my favorites for a truly unique portion of your wedding photos.

875. Talk with your photographer about some of the more original pictures you wish to have taken, such as you and your groom walking in the distance on the beach. Don't leave all the creative vision for your shots to your photographer! You're in charge of all aspects of your wedding, especially the lasting images of it. So play "stylist" and dream up the many romantic and wonderful shots you want for your day. Look through bridal magazines to copy the styles of *their* professionally set-up wedding images, and take tear-outs of those pictures to your photographer as a sample of what you're looking for.

876. Plan pictures that are completely *you*. You may be a fun-loving couple, so a picture of the two of you standing side by side isn't something that reflects your relationship. Him holding you from behind, with his chin on your shoulder—that looks more like you and the way you appear in real life. So plan your photos with that in mind. And don't be afraid to say *no* to your photographer if he or she is coming up with cheesy ideas. One bride tells me that her photographer thought it would be a *great* idea for her and her groom to stand next to a swimming pool and have him dip her backwards as if he were about to drop her into the pool. Unfortunately, she didn't have the nerve to say no to that idea, and while the groom kept his good grip on her, all she remembers is being terrified that she'd fall into the pool and be drenched before her reception even started. So stand your ground and feel free to veto any ideas that make you unhappy or uncomfortable.

877. Request pictures of you with your favorite people. While your photographer has a memorized list of the "usuals" (bride with her parents, groom with his parents, bride and groom with both sets of parents), you can and should ask for that shot of you with your favorite great-aunt, or more than a few pictures of you with your friends and your groom with his friends. Remember, you're not just immortalizing yourselves as a couple at the wedding. You know you were there. A good collection of wedding photos captures the day you spent with everyone you love.

878. Share the joy of your wedding photos by ordering or making separate photo albums for your parents and the groom's parents. Don't forget other special people like your godparents, your bridal party (why should they get only one or two photos from you when they were such a big part of your day?), your best friends, and if you have them in a newly blended family now, your kids.

879. Share your pictures online. There are more than a few online wedding photo-viewing and ordering sites out there, and most photographers arrange to put your pictures in a special account where others can view them and buy whichever prints they like. It's convenient, pictures often go up much more quickly than if you waited for proofs to be printed, and often they can eliminate the need for having proofs done at all! One of the best services out there right now is the award-winning www.collages.net (also at 267-572-5000), where you can have displays of your photos arranged into a CD or DVD slideshow, accompanied by a graceful music soundtrack.

880. Find great ways to display your wedding photos in your home. Very few people leave their official wedding albums out on the coffee table beyond the first year of the marriage. As much as you love it, it usually gets stowed away someplace safe. So look at great, unique frames at www.exposuresonline.com—you'll find natural wood frames, curved glass frames, even frames embedded with a microchip to record and play wording from the two of you (a portion of your wedding vows?) or your wedding song. Plus, as your décor changes over the years, you'll be happy that you have a mix of color and black and white pictures to match your future home decorating tastes.

881. The enormous advances in digital photography and editing options make creating your finished photo albums an art form. Wedding photographer Rich Penrose (my own wedding photographer) from Dean Michaels Studios in Madison, NJ, highly recommends that you look into the new effects afforded by digital artistry. "We can play with the picture, putting the couple in full color and the background in black and white, for instance." Or a red bouquet can stand out in color while everything else is black and white. Previously, these eye-catching effects were seen only in big-money magazine ads and in television commercials. Now they can quite easily be a part of your wedding album, and they can make your thank-you note portraits stand out.

882. Do something unique with your wedding portrait. Have a talented artist create a hand-drawn illustration of your picture, which can be displayed in your home or used for your thank-you notes. Hand-drawn copies of photographs are the new wave of personalized gifts.

Your Wedding Video

883. This is an area where some brides and grooms choose to save on their wedding budget and ask a friend to videotape the most important parts of their day on a personally owned camcorder. Of course, that's always an option, especially if you have a limited budget and you'd rather spend more on your flowers or your reception or your gown. But this choice is often one that brides and grooms *regret* after the fact. They wish they had better or more complete footage of their day, they wish they'd hired a professional, and they even feel bad about not having the money to hire one. So think hard before you choose to skip this mighty investment in your memories. You can never go back to the big day again, and it would be a shame to miss out on something so important to you.

884. Find a videographer whose style you admire. Again, it's all about the videographer's vision and the way he or she likes to capture the big moments. View plenty of samples, get referrals from friends, and most importantly, know what *you* want for your wedding video, rather than blindly walking into a studio and accepting what the videographer shows you. You should think ahead of time about whether you want your video to be a standard, or if you want it styled in the manner of a Madison Avenue perfume commercial, with plenty of scenery and gauzy special effects to make you both look like movie stars.

885. Editing in videos has come a long way. Professional video editors can splice and move footage to make your wedding "movie" flow like something worthy of the Sundance Film Festival.

886. Know which footage apart from the usuals that you want. Sure, you want tape of you dancing with your father, but you also might want footage of the groom looking across the room at you while you're dancing with your friends. An in-the-know videographer can set up that footage easily, capturing that admiring look in your groom's eyes as he watches you from a distance. It's exactly these kinds of nuances that are the *real* special moments of your day, and the best videographers know what to look for to capture them.

887. Don't forget the scenery. You want to capture *everything* about your day, so inform the videographer that you want a sweep of the landscape or a close-up of that great fountain in the circular driveway of the chateau where you're getting married. You chose that location for how it made you feel, and for what it would add to your wedding day. Having that scenery on tape to view in the future will only contribute to bringing you right back to that place in your memories.

888.
Take it easy on the special effects. You don't need an animated bunny hopping across your wedding footage, and you don't need strobe-light effects or other eye-rolling results from really bad special effects. Sit down with your videographer to ask about the various kinds of effects he or she can provide, and can show you right there on a computer screen. So many couples are not aware of the more subtle things a video editor can do with lighting, filters, and border work. You might be surprised, so don't be afraid to ask for a show of samples. The most popular effects are gauzy, soft-focus camerawork that looks like a dream sequence in a movie. Since this wedding is your dream come true, why not capture that effect in your video? Soft focus makes you look amazing on film, too.

889.
Want your wedding video to *really* look like a movie? Then ask your videographer to use a two- or three-camera system for your ceremony and reception. This is where each special element of your day from your ceremony to your first dance to your cake cutting is filmed simultaneously from two or three different angles, allowing changes in direction for the final version. It's a great way for the editor to capture all the action and get the very best shot for each special moment.

890. Make yours a video documentary of your wedding. Videographers are also calling themselves "videojournalists;" they are there to capture all the nuances of your day. Included in your footage might be great styled interviews with your guests—and not those old-fashioned segments where the videographer sneaks up on your guests at their tables, walking slowly around each one to film your guests waving into the camera or awkwardly grabbing a microphone to say a rushed "good luck!" to you. No, this newer version is more attention-to-detail than that. Special guests might be led over to a great couch or a terrace overlooking some great scenery, where they deliver a heartfelt message they've had some time to prepare for. Some videographers, after they've taken the cake-cutting footage, even set up a separate area with a director's chair and some flowers on the table nearby, calling it the Interview Room and inviting guests to drop in at their convenience to tape a message for you. This allows your guests to speak when they're ready, and from their hearts.

891. If you've ever seen the show *A Wedding Story* on TLC, you know that they end each segment with the bride and groom talking to one another about how great the day was and how happy they are to be married to one another. Copy that! Ask your videographer to interview the two of you after the wedding, right before you make your big getaway, so that you have your post-wedding glow and your new marriage bliss captured for posterity on tape.

892. And, of course, get copies of your video to give out to parents, grandparents, and other loved ones. They, too, would love a forever keepsake of your big day, and you might be surprised to find that they'll watch it just as often in the future, if not more often, than the two of you do! If not a video, get them a CD-ROM version to watch on their computers.

chapter 24

Getting a Ride

893. If you're looking for a traditional bridal ride in a limousine, consider a black limo rather than the usual white varieties. A black limo screams *"Celebrity!"* way more than a traditional white one, and photographers say that pictures of a bride stepping out of the car on her way to the ceremony come out *way* better with the black contrast behind her.

894. Of course, the new trend in wedding-day rides is skipping the limo and going for a classic car. Bentleys and Rolls Royces are most common, giving you that ultra-exorbitant feel, and they become more special because it's a once-in-a-lifetime ride—unless you're born into a rich and fabulous lifestyle where a Rolls is a big yawn.

895. Check out the wide variety in specialty and luxury cars by looking *specifically* for them. That means going online or to car shows where you'll find contacts for classic cars. Limo rental places don't often stock the unique cars, so you might miss out on the pickings if you go standard. Contact classic car clubs in your area to get the names and numbers of members who make a side living by renting out their "babies" for weddings. And those "babies" could even be something your groom loves: a stretch Humvee or Navigator, for instance—big time groom choices for their weddings. You'll be pleasantly surprised by the unique cars you'll find, and your guests will envy you when you pull up in something amazing and way more special than a limo.

896. If you're the carefree, adventurous types, rent or use your own convertible! Put the top down and decorate the car with a floral blanket and a big sign that says "Just Married." You often can't decorate limousines and rented classic cars like you can your own.

897. Speaking of decorating cars, check out the new static cling signs that you can attach to your car's windows and sides. These clear or colored strips announce "Just Married" or "Bride and Groom on Board" and then peel right off your car without leaving any marks or residue.

898. If your wedding will be on a beach or by a marina, arrive by boat. You can rent anything from a speedboat to a private yacht whose masts are strung with tiny white fairy lights for a surprising and special arrival, and then that "sailed off into the sunset" romantic finish.

899. Other couples who married on a beach, in a field, at an estate, or in the mountains made the most of "they rode off into the sunset" by arranging for two white horses to be on standby with their handlers, and once the ceremony was finished, they jumped up into the saddle and galloped away. Now that's a romantic departure—as well as a romantic arrival if the bride and/or groom make their approach on horseback.

900. And then we have the Harley crowd, couples who want to make their post-wedding getaways on the back of a motorcycle. Don't chalk this up to any stereotype, though. Many of today's motorcycles are gleaming masterpieces, especially those in bright colors and the black-and-chrome metallics that actually work quite well with your wedding's formality level. For the groom who lives to ride, or even the bride for that matter, this mode of transport can be truly *them*.

901. Also look into hot air balloons for a lift, or the romantic fantasy horse and carriage ride. Research well to find out about any permits you might need, weather or location restrictions carriage companies apply for the health and safety of their horses, and how you can arrange for the carriage driver to dress in something special: like a Victorian-era overcoat and hat. Most carriages come with an option to decorate them in a flower-strewn manner, complete with that must-have "Just Married" sign.

902. And, of course, there's always the party bus—the stocked-beyond-belief celebrity-style tour bus with leather seats, a great sound system, and mood lighting to transport your bridal party and family (and perhaps the two of you if you want to join the party on wheels) to and from the wedding and reception sites. This is a hugely popular idea for couples who have booked their weddings an hour's ride from their homes to make the most of a great location, or those where placating each side of the family means the ceremony is in one family's town and the reception in another. Rather than sweating transportation for all your most important players, book the party bus and let the after-party take place on board. Keep in mind that many companies that rent party buses have been known to bring them, sound systems blaring, to the parking lots of bridal expos and wedding showcases. So it could be a good idea to attend a few of these free shows in order to add "see party bus" to your list of things to research.

903. Don't forget that you might be able to wrangle use of the hotel's free shuttle bus as an added arrangement to your hotel booking, especially if your reception will take place at the hotel. Talk to the manager to see if you can arrange for their shuttle bus to transport guests to and from the ceremony and reception, remembering to book half-hourly stops at the reception hall for guests' individually preferred departure times. With permission, you can decorate the shuttle bus, have a personalized message displayed on its digital destination sign, or even stock the bus with bottles of water, soda, or snacks for one last happy surprise for your guests.

904. Speaking of drinks and snacks, you can also arrange to have your own car—whatever it may be—stocked with some water bottles, sodas, chips, snacks, or even champagne or wine if you'll be in a limousine (they're the only cars licensed to allow occupants to drink in while they're on the road).

905.

Also, make guests' transportation easier, especially if they'll be coming from out of town and arriving at airports or train stations. Either recruit the groomsmen to serve as chauffeurs, picking guests up in their own cars, or let guests know that you wish to pay for any taxi service they use. Whatever you can do to make your guests' arrival easier, do it.

chapter 25

A Place to Stay

Part of setting the scene for your entire wedding event also extends into the non-wedding hours. By that, I mean the places where you and your guests will spend a lot of time before and after the wedding events and perhaps even days before the wedding: your hotel rooms. While many brides and grooms in the past took care of this measure with just a quick phone call to the local hotel to reserve a block of rooms, the trend now is making your own and your guests' overnight stays something more special than just four walls, a bed, and a desk...great view optional. Here's how to perk up your lodging options and make all the days of your wedding event more of a vacation for all.

Your Own Room

906. While budget articles would tell you "Don't book the honeymoon suite" or a pricier hotel room, you can make your wedding morning and wedding night much more special by setting yourself up in a great penthouse or suite, rather than a dull business-class room with bad lighting and a lumpy bed. Instead, take a look at the hotel's luxury rooms, those with wet bars and leather couches, great décor and plenty of space, a hot tub, and a bathroom with terrific lighting and plenty of counter space where you can spread out your makeup on the morning of the wedding. Just stepping into a room this luxurious immediately sets the tone, and you'll agree that you *deserve* this great room on your big day.

907. Stock your room with the things that make you feel great: a silk robe, slippers, your favorite bubble bath. Make your own spa weekend getaway right there for the night before your wedding. See the end of Chapter 21 for more ideas on making the most of your honeymoon suite.

908. If you'd rather get away from the hotel where your wedding is being held or where all of your guests are staying, go to another hotel—perhaps a truly ritzy one where it's first class all the way.

909. Go with a cozier atmosphere by heading off to a bed and breakfast for the night. Okay, so you won't have the ultimate in privacy that first night with a dozen or so other guests in the house, but the atmosphere could be ideal with the Victorian poster bed, the fireplace in your bedroom, the great antiques filling the house, and the promise of fresh scones in the morning. One groom wrote to me that he made his bride's most romantic wish come true by booking their wedding night at a bed and breakfast. His bride had always dreamt about spending her wedding night in a room that had a fireplace, where she and her groom would sit in front of the fire to cuddle and sip champagne. Well, the groom looked everywhere for a hotel that had a room with the fireplace in it, and he had no luck. So he went online, found a nearby bed and breakfast, scoped it out, and booked it as a surprise for his bride. He had her luggage brought from the hotel room where she got ready that morning to their new destination (the bed and breakfast), unpacked for her, *and* had the gift of a new monogrammed robe (with her new married initials) waiting for her in the room at the end of the night. Now that's a special memory provided by the groom's choice of location for their first night as husband and wife.

Rooms for Guests

910. If you'll have out-of-town guests for your wedding, it's wise to do what so many other brides and grooms regularly do and arrange for a block of rooms to be reserved for them at one hotel. You can reserve rooms at the hotel where the wedding will be held, *or* allow guests their choice of rooms ready for booking at a family-style hotel or at a more upscale hotel nearby. Giving guests a choice allows them to go with their comfort level, perhaps see their trip to your wedding as their *vacation* (especially if you reserve at a resort that offers spa treatments, skiing, swimming pool, and beach access), and it also allows your guests on a more moderate budget to reserve a spot that works better for them. I hear too many wedding guests complaining that they'll have to drive two hours to get to the wedding, and then drive home two hours after the wedding since they just couldn't swing that $300 a night at the ritzy hotel where the wedding couple reserved rooms for their guests. Of course, they're free to look up more moderately priced hotels in the area, but why make them do all the work? You'll be a gracious host if you simply list the two different hotels for your guests' choice. But beware: don't actually write any indicators like "low-budget hotel" or "fancy hotel" on the lodgings info card you send. Some guests' egos could get stomped when they find themselves having to book the "low-budget hotel." Just simply provide the names of the hotels and let guests take it from there.

A Thoughtful Detail

911. Make guests feel welcome by placing a goodie-filled bag or basket in each of their hotel rooms. Include bottles of water and soda (so no one has to look for a convenience store or pay top-dollar at the hotel's gift shop), snacks, even travel-sized pampering products like skin creams or aromatherapy spritzers. Here are a number of additional ideas for your guests' goodie baskets:

• Cans of soda—regular, diet, and caffeine-free (some people have a preference!)
• Bottles of juice
• Mini bags of crackers or healthy snack mix
• Gum and breath mints
• Guidebooks or pamphlets to nearby sites of interest
• New magazines for downtime reading
• Travel-sized pampering items (such as skin lotions)
• Fuzzy slippers
• A reminder set of printed directions to the rehearsal and the wedding locations
• Games and toys for the kids
• Add a welcome note from the two of you, and start your guests' arrival off right

912. Of course, it's a wonderful idea to welcome guests to their hotel with a cocktail party waiting just for them. You can arrange for an hour's worth of welcome drinks and *hors d'oeuvres* or a cheese and fruit platter in a private party out by the pool, for your wedding guests only, or even a welcome brunch if your people will be arriving earlier in the day.

913. Even better, if guests will be staying more than one day, such as an extended wedding weekend, have a separate goodie bag or food treat sent to their rooms as a surprise the next night. Some couples will have a complimentary bottle of wine sent up to their friends who are couples, or treats like fresh cookies and milk sent up to rooms where kids are staying.

914. Research ahead of time any special events that will be taking place at the guests' hotel. Many resorts print up a list of guided kids' activities, such as sandcastle building contests, arts and crafts, or the showing of movies in the kids' lounge. Making sure that families have something for their kids to do is a great way to welcome them.

915. Have a contingency plan for guests who, for some reason, can't stay at the hotel. Having just left one resort early due to very loud music coming up through the vents from the lounge during a Friday night, as well as room service closing down an hour early, *and* the hotel's cable being out (I'll never stay there again!), I know that the best-laid plans can often go awry. So be sure to have a nearby relative or friend on standby to host late-arriving guests who find that they just can't stay in the hotel. This is the kind of thing where forethought can save the day. So ask ahead of time if anyone would be willing to host should the need arise.

chapter 26

Wedding Weekend Plans

Making weddings *way* more special these days is the advent of the stretched-out wedding weekend, three or four days filled with lots of group activities that allow you and your guests lots of downtime and fun outings where you can spend more quality time together. It used to be that you would just see your out-of-town friends *during* your wedding, probably getting ten minutes total of catching-up time before someone would drag you away to say hello to Aunt Esther. Now, you get lots more time to see everyone who's traveled in to share your day with you. They could be friends who've moved away for work or relationships or family you haven't seen in years. At some weddings, the bride finally gets to see her old college roommate's new baby for the first time, or her three kids if it's really been a while. These wedding weekends are just priceless in terms of making a wedding special, since they're all about spending time with your favorite people.

916. When planning wedding weekend activities, look first at meals. Mix up a sit-down dinner one night with a more informal barbecue at your parents' place another night. You could plan an afternoon picnic out at the park to coincide with a more playful event (more on that in a minute), and even invite your friends only out for sushi one evening while your parents entertain their friends separately.

917. Then there's always going out for drinks with your friends and family who are up for a late night out, or just for a fun happy hour. Some brides and grooms love spending time out with their friends and their cousins and their coworkers, just going out for a relaxed night of toasts and laughter.

918. Next up are activities. Team sports are usually the thing, pitting His Side versus Her Side in everything from softball to flag football, miniature golf, and even bowling. Choose a sport your guests would love to participate in, and create a tournament complete with a trophy for the winning team.

919. For your more adventurous guests, arrange for something a little more exciting and blood-pumping. It could be adventure sports like kayaking or horseback riding on the beach—something your friends and family don't often get to do. Other ideas include Jet Skiing, snowboarding, mountain biking, or hiking through waterfall areas.

920. Look at seasonal events. For example, a beach trip is in order if you're anywhere near the ocean or a lake during the summer months. In the autumn, lead your caravan to a big family farm where they offer hayrides out to the pumpkin patches, petting zoos, fruit-picking in the orchards, and the most popular attraction at these family farms across the country: corn mazes.

921. Grab everyone and head out to a winery for a tour and wine tasting. Remember, you're making this a fun vacation for them and a good investment in their travel and lodging dollars. Planning fun, out-of-the-ordinary activities your guests will love is a smart move, and gives you new memories (and great pictures) to last a long time.

922. Another popular activity for wedding weekends is sending guests off on a historical tour of your city. You love your adopted home city, and you want to show the best parts of it to your friends and family. So, while you're off picking up your wedding gown and your groom is getting his tuxedo, all of your guests are entertained on a professionally led walking or bus tour of the attractions in your area. Look into these tours. Depending on the size of the city where you live, you might find tours such as:

- historic tours such as American Revolution battlefields or former presidents' homes
- tours of places where some famous movies were filmed
- celebrity home tours
- tours of Victorian mansions (especially during the winter holidays when they're all decorated and open to the public)
- culinary tours with a stop to eat at some famous restaurants with fabulous chefs
- haunted tours of war-era homes that are supposedly haunted by ghosts

It's going to be an adventurous outing for those guests of yours who are willing to attend, and everyone else gets downtime by the pool or the freedom to plan their own little side trips.

923. Invite the women to a day spa for an afternoon of pampering, and let the men watch the playoffs at the sports bar.

924. Family outings can be just the ticket for guests who have kids. Check out local listings of family events coming up, such as town carnivals and festivals, or look up children's museums, aquariums, and perhaps even just a great playground in a local park where you can host a giant picnic and softball game for the adults.

925. Movie nights are great for a crowd. Prepurchase a block of tickets to the local movie theater, or a drive-in movie theater if there's one by you, and take in the latest family film.

chapter 27

A Token of Appreciation

With so many special people participating in your wedding (including the two of you!), it's a wise and wonderful move to give them back a little something special—a favor or gift that thanks them for their help or their presence.

Wedding Favors

Edibles

926. The most appreciated favor is something your guests can eat and enjoy. So choose from the following ideas:

- Wrapped chocolates or truffles are a delicious and sophisticated gift. Nothing beats the upscale elegance of Godiva two-piece or four-piece chocolate boxes with theme ribbon or imprinted ribbon from www.godiva.com.

- If you're looking at truffles, flip through a catalog or visit a chocolatier website to check out the many unique flavors. You'll find flavors that are your all-time favorites, or flavors that work with your wedding's theme or location, such as a key lime truffle for your Florida Keys destination wedding.

- At chocolate shops, you'll also find cute shapes and themes in their personally created line of goodies. You can then hand out white chocolate hearts or white chocolate snowflakes to work with your theme.

- Also popular are chocolate-dipped goodies like pretzels, nuts, fruits, and even coffee beans. Package these in a cute box or tulle bag for great presentation of a sweet treat.

- Use candy-making or lollipop kits found at your local craft store to melt your own chocolate and custom-design your own chocolate creations. You'll find great theme molds, such as stars, hearts, roses, daisies, moons, racecars, footballs, and other outlines.

Simple, Pretty, and Delicious

Extremely popular right now are simple, frosted cookies in a small batch wrapped in tulle or protected in pretty gift boxes. One of my absolute favorite sources is Cheryl&Company (www.cherylandco.com), where you'll find cookies expertly frosted in colors that can work with your wedding's décor, such as lemon yellow, pale green (their Frosted Key Lime White Chip cookie), baby pink, soft orange (their Frosted Orange Citrus), bridal white—even a bright orange pumpkin or red and green holiday frostings to work with your holiday-themed wedding. Here's just a sampling of their great cookie flavors for the ultimate in edible wedding favors:

Chocolate chip	Oatmeal raisin
White chocolate chip	Sugar cookie
Pecan chocolate chip	Spice
Oatmeal chocolate chip	Peanut butter
Cashew chocolate chip	Peanut butter with nuts
Macadamia white chocolate chip	Chocolate chunk

Or look to Cheryl&Company's collection of brownies, also packaged smartly in gift boxes or protective containers. A sampling of brownie flavors are:

Fudge	Blondies
Raspberry crumb	Macadamia
Coconut toffee crunch	Oatmeal Scotchie
Chocolate coconut almond	Chocolate kiss
LemonCool Key lime	Chocolate caramel pecan
Chocolate curl	Peanut butter cup

They also offer frosted gingerbread shapes for a holiday weddings.

• Although the small wine bottles with personalized labels are going out of style in favor of real vintages with the honor of their own labels, this concept is still working for some couples who do it right. One idea is to select a vintage that's from your heritage country, like an Australian wine or a New Zealand wine, a French Merlot, or an Italian dessert wine. Check www.winespectator.com for detailed reviews and suggestions.

Living Favors

927. It's quite symbolic to give your guests something that will bloom and grow, just like your marriage! So check out the following ideas:

• Potted plants and seedlings are great gifts. Choose between potted baby rosebuds, daisies, tulips, orchids, and other flowers, clover, or ivy. For each potted flowering plant or green plant, wrap the base with colored foil and then label it with growing directions and a personal note of thanks.

• Potted herb plants are also on the rise, with rosemary leading the pack of great living favor options. Lavender, too, is a big one for the giveaway, especially if its light purple color goes with your décor.

• Flower seeds are another popular gift. Put wildflower seeds in a tulle pouch, and then add a label with a quote such as "Those who plant kindness harvest love."

- Mini bamboo shoot plants are also a hot favor right now. Check at your florist or nursery for these very popular potted collections of four to six bamboo lengths, or the more expensive "curly bamboo" that's been shaped into a spiral.

Items to Keep and Use

928. Of course, you can give your guests something functional that they will use often, and that also might add to the décor of their home:

- Candles and candleholders.
- Glass hurricane lamps with color-coordinated pillar candles.
- Glass potpourri bowls with a signature scent of potpourri, such as rose or gardenia, or an ocean scent.
- Silver frames, found in craft stores or in bulk from great low-priced sources such as Pier 1 Imports (www.pier1.com) where I found adorable butterfly-themed silver frames for under ten dollars apiece.
- Glass bowls filled with sand, seashells, and a silver starfish necklace on a string.
- Books of romantic poetry, images, or quotes—for an added personal touch, include a homemade bookmark imprinted with your names and wedding date.

- Videotapes or DVDs—I *love* this idea from a couple in Chicago who gave out to their guests copies of the first romantic movie the couple ever saw together. Choose a variety of romantic movies your guests might not already own, providing a mix of VHS and DVDs, and let your guests choose their own favorites.

- CD Mixes—Use your own home computer to burn romantic or memory-laden music mix CDs for your guests, and then use CD jackets and labels found at your local office supply store to personalize the packaging. Again, this is one option your guests will love…and use again and again (unlike a brandy snifter with your names inscribed on it).

- Ornaments—Buy beautiful color-coordinated or white ornaments from a local craft store, and either wrap them in tulle or set them in pretty see-through plastic boxes with a personalized note.

- Pampering products, such as baskets filled with hand creams, body lotions, face blotting papers, a loofah sponge, and other spa-type goodies

- Fun items for theme weddings—For your beach wedding, for instance, hand out colorful sand buckets containing sunglasses, sunscreen, lip sunblock, a trashy paperback novel, and a packet of iced tea mix for a fun gift under $25 that will be used again. For winter weddings, give out mugs with snowmen on them, packets of hot chocolate mix, a baggie of marshmallows, and perhaps pairs of fun, brightly-colored gloves or mittens.

Additional Ideas

929. Be sure to label the adults' and children's favors separately. Especially if you're giving out bottles of wine or liqueur-filled chocolates, you wouldn't want the kids to grab those by mistake (or on purpose, if they're teenagers!). If you're getting separate kids' favors, make sure they're of an easily identifiable shape or displayed separately.

930. Attach a preprinted or handwritten note of thanks to each favor, signed with your names.

931. Arrange the favors on a special table near the exit for your guests' own selection.

932. Arrange the favors in the centers of the guest tables as a double-duty, inexpensive alternative to a pricier centerpiece. Those beautifully tulle-wrapped candles will make attractive accents to your table décor.

Gifts to Give Others

Gifts for Bride and Groom to Give One Another

Certainly, the most important and special gifts you'll give are the ones you and your groom exchange with one another. You'll keep this present forever, and even the most sentiment-averse groom on earth knows that he'd better knock this one out of the park by choosing something special and meaningful for his bride. Here are some of the most popular ideas for gifts brides and grooms can give one another right before or after the wedding.

933. Most grooms give their brides special wedding day jewelry, such as diamond earrings or a diamond necklace, a set of pearl jewelry, or a silver charm bracelet that's special to the bride. The bride might give her groom a top-quality watch for him to wear on the big day as well. His and hers engraved watches are also way up there on the list of couple presents.

934. For a romantic sentiment that shows your partner how important you consider him to be, present him with all of his love letters that you've kept as treasure, tied with a red ribbon.

935. Give your partner an ultra-fine bottle of wine to be shared on your first wedding anniversary. It's a gift for now and a promise for the future.

936. Show that you support one another's goals and accomplishments. I've heard from several brides that they cried when their grooms presented them with professionally framed copies of their greatest awards, such as a diploma or a letter of acceptance to a prestigious school, program, or club.

937. Another way to show support of your intended's most important goals is to help them on their way. For instance, you might purchase the gift of an entry fee and travel expenses to a high-level business conference (as in, "There's this conference my fiancé has always wanted to go to, but it's in Hawaii, and he only dreams of being able to go someday." Set him up now!), a leather portfolio, or something that really starts your beloved off in the right direction. A recent bride wrote in to share this story:

"Since the day I met Jeff, he's been talking about his plan to open up his own chiropractor practice. He has sketches of the kinds of wallpaper he wants for his office, pictures torn out of catalogs for the kind of desk he wants.... When I asked him why he didn't pursue it, he said he hasn't found the right location yet. One day, we were out at a street festival a few towns over from where we live, and Jeff saw the perfect storefront. And it was for lease! So I wrote down the name and number of the realtor, called, looked at it, had experts come in to assess its structure, and I paid for six months' leasing of that ideal place in advance. I almost got caught, too. Jeff asked me where the name and number of that realtor was, because he wanted to go check out the place, and I said I couldn't find the number. The day before our wedding, I drove him out there and handed him the key. I LOVED being able to make him so happy, and he was!"

938.

It's not the lease to a dream come true, but it captures your past, present and future: Give a photo album featuring pictures of the two of you during your courtship…and leave the last half of the book empty and waiting for future snapshots of you through the years. Slide in a note explaining: *The rest of this book awaits, as I do, the many happy moments and memories of our wonderful future together.*

Gifts for the Groomsmen and Best Man

Man-appropriate gifts come in a wide range of options, from something to own and use to some event to enjoy. Consider the following ideas to see which ones work best with your particular group of guys.

939. Give each man several fine cigars to enjoy after a round of golf or at the after-party.

940. Buy a gift certificate for a round of golf at a nearby country club or public course.

941. Giving your men tickets to a sporting event, especially if it's a playoff game or the World Series, makes *you* an all-time hero.

942. Give him a great night out with tickets to a concert by a musical performer he likes. (Even better, get the whole group tickets to one great concert or music festival so you can all go together!)

943. Give everyone tickets to a great comedy club (again for a group night out), or tickets to a prize-winning theater production.

944. Frame a picture of your group of friends.

945. Get something engraved, such as:

- Silver flasks
- Money clips
- Cuff links
- Watches
- Beer mugs
- Silver key chains
- Silver business card cases

946. For a classic touch, give each man a silver shaving kit.

947. Create a professionally edited videotape of your best moments together over the years.

948. Give each of your men a bottle of fine port, brandy or cognac—with a note promising each that you'll get together for toasts on all special occasions in the future.

949. Give him a gift certificate to a fine restaurant, so that your guy can take *his* girl out for a romantic night on the town. Consider it an investment in his love life and future happiness as well.

Gifts for the Bridesmaids and Maid of Honor

Of course, your lovely ladies deserve a gift as well.

950. Give jewelry to wear on the wedding day: necklaces, bracelets, or earring and necklace sets in the gemstone color you wish for them to wear, or in an all-purpose and future use silver.

951. Get engraved items such as:

- Silver bracelets or heart locket necklaces
- Silver business card cases
- Silver compact (one of my favorites, found at www.thingsremembered.com)

952. Initial necklaces in silver or gold, with or without a diamond chip embedded in the letter are very hot.

953. Your women will love receiving a very fine perfume, along with a lotion set in the same scent.

954. Pamper her with a satin robe and slippers set from Victoria's Secret.

955. Give her a beautiful silver picture frame with your favorite picture of the two of you. Make that picture frame even more special by choosing a double picture frame that holds both a picture of you from when you were little girls and a current photo from the wedding day.

956. For a fun night out, give each of your bridesmaids tickets to a play or concert by their favorite performer.

957. As the perfect, useful keepsake, give each of your bridesmaids a personalized jewelry box, with a monogram or engraving on the top.

958. Create a professionally edited videotape of your growing-up years together and all of your most memorable times captured on tape.

959. Make a music mix CD reminiscent of all your favorite songs that bring back great memories for you both.

960. Give a gift certificate to a bookstore or bookstore café or a copy of a book she would love, signed by the author. (You can either acquire this autographed version yourself at a big city booksigning, or call a local bookstore where the author appeared recently. They often keep extra signed copies on hand, and will be happy to send one to you, or ship it to a store closer to you.) Bookstores are also often willing to ask the publisher to get a copy signed, but be aware this can take several weeks.

961. Give your bridesmaids something personalized, even whimsical, to display in their homes, such as a handmade craft item like a needlepoint pillow with your favorite quote or catchphrase.

962. A collection of wonderful, scented pillar candles (or feng shui candles if your friends are into that sort of thing) helps your bridesmaid create that romantic and relaxing look for her home or bedroom.

963. Give her the gift of a promised toast in the future by giving her a bottle of fine wine or champagne to be shared on a special occasion.

964. Give each of your bridesmaids an appointment book with a future date circled as the weekend you'll go away for a girls' road trip. This special gift assures your friends that you will never leave them behind, you won't change, and you'll always make time for them.

Gifts for Parents

Whenever you choose to give it to them—whether the night before the wedding, at the rehearsal dinner, or on the morning of the wedding— a great gift for your parents shows them how much you appreciate them. Choose from the following ideas, or come up with something special on your own.

965. Give them special jewelry items, such as a mother's ring with your birthstone in it.

966. Engraved watches with a love message from you on the back are a thoughtful gift.

967. Find a great bottle of wine or champagne for her and a bottle of fine cognac or port for him.

968. Purchase tickets to:

• A concert by their favorite musical or comedy artist
• The opera
• A Broadway play
• A sporting event for a team they both love

969. To give them the break they need after all their help planning the wedding, buy them a weekend getaway at a hotel or resort.

970. Engrave a silver picture frame to hold wedding day portraits of you with your parents.

971. A newly designed photo album featuring pictures of them throughout the years, or photos of your family.

972. Purchase a professionally edited videotape of your family's old home movies, with a soundtrack of their favorite songs.

973. Give your parents a professionally edited videotape of *their* childhood days, or stills of their childhood snapshots, continuing up through to the present day. If your parents' footage goes way back to Super-8 film reels, you can have old family reels transferred to video or DVD now.

974. A simple, yet wonderful idea is to write a heartfelt letter to tell your parents all the specific things you're so grateful that they taught you, special memories of your growing-up years that you'll always hold dear, and a new chance to tell your parents that you love them. This often is the best choice, the one most parents will truly get teary-eyed over.

Gifts for Kids

For your flower girls and ringbearers, or your own kids if you are blending your two groups of children into one family, it's a wonderful idea to give the children a special gift on the wedding day. Here are some ideas to consider.

975. Give a special piece of jewelry, such as a diamond pendant, an engraved silver charm bracelet or ID bracelet, or an engraved watch for older children

976. Children will love a music box with the child's favorite character inside (like Snow White, Cinderella, or Barbie).

977. Purchase a much wanted item that the kids have been wanting (or that the kids' parents have okayed), such as new skis, a certificate for new sports lessons such as karate or dance classes, or a new TV for their bedroom.

978. Give tickets to the hottest teen concert coming through town, or to a Broadway play or professional figure skating performance—whatever the child's passion is.

979. A gift certificate for a shopping trip for new clothing, with parental veto power in play, or to a music or bookstore, allows kids to pick out exactly what they want.

980. Purchase a makeover at a day spa or salon. Today's new spas and salons feature teen-appropriate facial treatments, massages, haircuts, and manicures. For a pre-teen or teenager in your bridal party, this one is ideal.

981. For the sports fan, find tickets to a playoff game or a professional regular-season game. Give the tickets along with a team-logo tee shirt or hat.

Registering for Gifts

Of course, there are the many gifts that you will receive yourselves from guests at your showers, engagement parties, and your wedding. Here are a few tips for making sure you get all the special things that you want for your future.

Everyone's Doing It

For a look at how other brides and grooms are approaching their registries, we'll turn one last time to the survey from *WeddingBells* magazine:

- 71 percent of engaged couples will attend four or more parties in the months leading up to their wedding day
- 19 percent report that they will attend an astonishing ten or more parties up to their weddings
- 89 percent plan to register at two or more stores
- 67 percent will register at department stores
- 50 percent expect to get most if not all of what they register for

And the top registry items are:
- 76 percent - Cookware and bakeware
- 74 percent - Linens
- 69 percent - Small appliances
- 67 percent - Casual dinnerware
- 63 percent - Flatware and cutlery
- 58 percent - Crystal and stemware
- 40 percent - China and formal dinnerware

982. Be sure to register for a range of gift prices, so that your guests on lower budgets aren't tempted to go off your list and get you what they *think* you might like since they can't afford the pricier things you list on your registry.

983. Register for a mix of household items and items that work with your interests. Many couples are registering for mountain bikes and kayaks, for instance, to allow them to enjoy their active lifestyle together as a team.

984. Home improvement concepts are also hot on couples' registry lists, so look at Home Depot and Lowe's for their registries of power tools, painting supplies, outdoor needs like gardening tools and ladders, leaf blowers, window treatments, and everything you need to make over your outdoor deck.

985. Honeymoon registries allow guests to contribute to your trip, or to special dinners and activities you'll enjoy on your trip. Some travel agencies maintain registries where guests can give you the gift of a scuba excursion or a champagne dinner cruise while you're in Aruba or St. Lucia, or fill your cruise cabin with flowers upon your arrival.

986. Look at registries with a charitable touch, such as the I Do Foundation (www.IDOFoundation.org), where you sign up, guests participate, and a portion of the proceeds go to worthy causes. Or, if you have everything you need for your home, you can encourage your guests to give donations to their favorite causes—in lieu of wedding gifts to you—by visiting www.justgive.org.

987. Make it easy for guests to get to your registry by listing it on your own wedding website (see www.wedstudio.com to sign up for your own personal site).

chapter 28

Making the Last Moments Count

988. Videotape everything! You'll be in a blur, and days will fly by. So make sure you have someone working the video camera to capture everything that goes on at the rehearsal and the rehearsal dinner, last-day dinners, and especially the night before the wedding when you and your groom can record special messages to one another. This footage makes for great keepsakes!

989. On the night before your wedding, see if you and your groom would like to enact the old tradition that you won't see each other on the day of the wedding until you meet at the altar. If that's the case, make plans to spend the night apart—although you can talk for hours on the phone throughout the night.

990. Each of you can make a video greeting to one another, in which you'll speak your heart to your intended on the night before your wedding. When you go to your own separate quarters for the night, you'll both watch each other's messages and be free to wipe away those tears of joy in private.

991. Spend some time talking with your parents. This is an emotional time for them. They may feel like they're losing you, especially if you plan to move far away after the wedding. So make a date with them for late-night coffee and talking time. Nothing else on your to-do list is more important than this planned together time with them.

992. The same goes for your siblings. If Mom and Dad turn in early on a regular basis, perhaps you and your sister or brother can go out for some coffee or a quick drink to spend some time together.

993. Make sure you're packed. Have your checklist in hand, and see that you have everything from your airline tickets to your passport to enough underwear to get you through your honeymoon.

994. Spend some time alone. You might want to take a bath, go for a run, write in your journal, or just chill out as you think about the wonder and blessings of the life transition you're about to embark upon. One bride wrote in to say that she went off by herself to sit in her church and just spent some time alone. Another went out to her backyard and sat on her old childhood swing set (the one her nieces now used) to smile to herself about her great luck. Give yourself a moment like these.

995. Grooms, now's the time to order flowers to be delivered to your bride the next morning, so she can awaken to your thoughtful gesture, or arrange to have a gift or card sent to her at the salon or hotel suite where she'll prepare for the wedding. Brides, same goes for you if you would like a card or gift sent to your groom on the wedding morning.

996. It's also a smart and thoughtful move to arrange to have flowers sent to your parents on the day *after* the wedding as a gesture of thanks.

Finally, get some sleep! You're going to need it for tomorrow!

On the Day of the Wedding

997. Have a special breakfast with your family. This family breakfast is taking the place of the bridal brunch, as more and more couples are deciding that they'd rather have an hour alone with their absolute closest to start off the day. Of course, you can always go for a light breakfast with your family and still have that bridal brunch, to make the most of your getting-ready time together.

998. Countless grooms have started off the morning of their wedding by playing golf or touch football with their buddies, so why not go off with the guys for a round or a game? Keep yourself busy, keep those nerves at bay, and enjoy the lasting memories of your final hours as a single person.

999. Some brides like to take off with their best friends to get a quick massage at a spa, and this idea is even picking up with grooms these days. Work the kinks out of your neck, and you'll be ultra-relaxed and ready to start the day.

1000. Now is the perfect time to give your parents and other close family and friends a heartfelt card or gift from you, with a nice letter. This kind of gesture makes these last moments extra special. If you have kids, spend some private time alone with them this morning, too. Go out to breakfast, spend time talking about how excited you all are, and remind the kids that you love them.

Now, you're on your way to make your wedding truly special for the two of you, and for everyone who's lucky enough to know you and share your big day with you. It's my hope that you've found plenty of inspiring ideas in this book, and have been further inspired to dream up your own symbolic and sentimental touches for your wedding of a lifetime.

Thank you for allowing me to be a part of your planning experience, and I wish you an overflowing abundance of love, luck, happiness, and health in your future together! May all of your days together be wonderful, and may you always look for creative ways to remind one another of how special and how important you are to one another.

If you would like to share your wonderful planning ideas with me for inclusion in future editions of this book, or in any of my upcoming wedding books or articles, please visit me at www.sharonnaylor.net and email your experiences directly to me. If I use your real-life wedding story in an upcoming title, I will quote you and send you a copy of the book in which your name appears.

All the best,
Sharon Naylor

Additional Books
by Sharon Naylor

The Mother of the Groom Book

1000 Best Wedding Bargains

Your Special Wedding Toasts

Your Special Wedding Vows

The Groom's Guide

Your Day, Your Way: The Essential Handbook for the 21st Century Bride, co-authored with celebrity bridal gown designers Michelle and Henry Roth

The Ultimate Bridal Shower Idea Book

The New Honeymoon Planner

How to Have a Fabulous Wedding for $10,000 or Less

The Complete Outdoor Wedding Planner

How to Plan an Elegant Wedding in 6 Months or Less

The Mother of the Bride Book

1001 Ways to Have a Dazzling Second Wedding

The 52 Most Romantic Places In and Around New York City (Contributor)

and others as listed at www.sharonnaylor.net

Resources

Please note that contact information does change with the advent of new area codes and changes in Internet addresses. All contact information was current at the time of this publication and we apologize if such a change has occurred since the publication of this book.

Bed and Breakfasts

Bed and Breakfasts, Country Inns, and Small Hotels:
    www.virtualcities.com/ons/Oonsadex.htm
Bed and Breakfast International Guide:
    www.ibbp.com
Fodors: www.fodors.com

Bridal Gowns

Alfred Angelo: 800-531-1125,
www.alfredangelo.com

America's Bridal Discounters: 800-326-0833,
www.bridaldiscounters.com

Amsale: 212-971-0170, www.amsale.com

Birnbaum and Bullock: 212-242-2914,
www.birnbaumandbullock.com

Bonny: 800-528-0030, www.bonny.com

Bridal Originals: 800-876-GOWN,
www.bridaloriginals.com

Brides-R-Us.com: 800-598-0685,
www.brides-r-us.com

Christos, Inc.: 212-921-0025; www.christosbridal.com

David's Bridal: 800-399-BRIDE,
www.davidsbridal.com

Demetrios: 212-967-5222, www.demetriosbride.com

Diamond Collection: 212-302-0210,
www.diamondbride.com

Eden Bridals: 800-828-8831, www.edenbridals.com
(check out their values collection!)

Emme Bridal Inc.: 281-634-9225,
www.emmebridal.com

Forever Yours Intl. Corp.: 631-951-4500,
www.foreverbridals.com

Galina: 212-564-1020, www.galinabridal.com

Gowns Online: www.gownsonline.com

Group USA: www.groupusa.com

Janell Berté: 717-291-9894, www.berte.com

Jasmine: 800-634-0224, www.jasminebridal.com

Jessica McClintock: 800-333-5301,
    www.jessicamcclintock.com
Jim Hjelm: 800-686-7880, www.jimhjelmvisions.com
Lila Broude: 212-921-8081
Manalé: 212-944-6939, www.manale.com
Marisa: 212-944-0022, www.marisabridals.com
Melissa Sweet Bridal Collection: 404-633-4395,
    www.melissasweet.com
Michelle Roth: 212-245-3390, www.michelleroth.com
Mon Cheri: 609-530-1900, www.mcbridals.com
Mori Lee: 212-840-5070, www.morilee.com
Priscilla of Boston: 617-242-2677,
    www.priscillaofboston.com
Private Label by G: 800-858-3338,
    www.privatelabelbyg.com
Roaman's Romance (Plus-Sizes): 800-436-0800
Sweetheart: 800-223-6061, www.gowns.com
Tomasina: 412-563-7788, www.tomasinabridal.com
Venus: 800-OH-VENUS
Vera Wang: 212-575-6400, www.verawang.com
Yumi Katsura: 212-772-3760, www.yumikatsura.com

Bridal Shows and Conferences

Bridal Show Producers International (find a bridal
    show near you): www.bspishows.com
Great Bridal Expo: 800-422-3976,
    www.bridalexpo.com

Bridesmaids' and Mother of the Bride Gowns

After Six: 800-444-8304, www.aftersix.com

Alfred Angelo: 800-531-1125, www.alfredangelo.com

Bill Levkoff: 800-LEVKOFF, www.billlevkoff.com

Chadwick's of Boston Special Occasions:
    800-525-6650

Champagne Formals: 212-302-9162,
    www.champagneformals.com

David's Bridal: 888-399-BRIDE,
    www.davidsbridal.com

Dessy Creations: www.dessy.com

JC Penney: 800-222-6161, www.jcpenney.com

Jessica McClintock: 800-333-5301,
    www.jessicamcclintock.com

Jim Hjelm Occasions: 800-686-7880,
    www.jimhjelmoccasions.com

Lazaro: 212-764-5781, www.lazarobridal.com

Macy's: 877-622-9274,
    www.macys.weddingchannel.com

Melissa Sweet Bridal Collection: 404-633-4395,
    www.melissasweet.com

Mori Lee: 212-840-5070, www.morileeinc.com

Silhouettes: www.silhouettesmaids.com

Spiegel: 800-527-1577, www.spiegel.com

Vera Wang: 800-VEW-VERA, www.verawang.com

Watters and Watters: 972-960-9884,
    www.watters.com

Cake Supplies
Wilton: 800-794-5866, www.wilton.com

Calligraphy
Calligraphy by Kristen:
  www.calligraphybykristen.com
Petals and Ink: 818-509-6783, www.petalsnink.com

Cameras
Cameras 101: www.cameras101.com
C&G Disposable Cameras:
  www.cngdisposablecamera.com
Custom Disposable Cameras:
  www.custom-disposable-cameras.com
Kodak: 800-242-2424, www.kodak.com
Michaels: www.michaels.com
Occasion Cameras: www.occasioncameras.com
Wedding Party Pack: 800-242-2424

Ceremony Sites
USA Citylink: www.usacitylink.com

Children's Wedding Wear
David's Bridal: 888-399-2743, www.davidsbridal.com
Finetica Child: www.Fineticachild.com
Katie and Co.: www.katieco.com
Posie's: www.posies.com
Storybook Heirlooms: www.storybookonline.com

Fabrics

Fabric Depot: 800-392-3376, www.fabricdepot.com

Fabric Mart: 800-242-3695

Greenberg and Hammer: 800-955-5135

Favors and Gifts

Chandler's Candle Company: 800-463-7143,
    www.chandlerscandle.com

Exclusively Weddings: 800-759-7666,
    www.exclusivelyweddings.com

Favors by Serendipity: 800-320-2664,
    www.favorsbyserendipity.com

Forever and Always Company: 800-404-4025,
    www.foreverandalways.com

Gift Emporia.com: www.giftemporia.com

Godiva: 800-9-GODIVA, www.godiva.com

Gratitude: 800-914-4342, www.giftsofgratitude.com

Illuminations: www.illuminations.com

Personal Creations: 800-326-6626

Pier 1: 800-245-4595, www.pier1.com

Seasons: 800-776-9677

Service Merchandise: 800-251-1212,
    www.servicemerchandise.com

Things Remembered: 800-274-7367,
    www.thingsremembered.com

Tree and Floral Beginnings (seedlings, bulbs, and
    candles): 888-315-7333, www.plantamemory.com

Wireless: 800-669-9999

Flowers

About.com: www.about.com

Association of Specialty Cut Flower Growers:
440-774-2887, www.ascfg.org

Flowersales.com: www.flowersales.com

International Floral Picture Database:
www.flowerweb.com

Romantic Flowers: www.romanticflower.com

Hotels and Resorts

Beaches: 800-BEACHES

Club Med: www.clubmed.com

Disney: www.disneyweddings.com

Hilton Hotels: www.hilton.com

Hyatt Hotels: www.hyatt.com

Marriott Hotels: www.marriott.com

Radisson: www.radisson.com

Sandals: 888-SANDALS, www.sandals.com

Super Clubs: 877-GO-SUPER, www.superclubs.com

Westin Hotels: www.westin.com

Invitations

An Invitation to Buy – Nationwide:
www.invitations4sale.com

Anna Griffin Invitation Design: 404-817-8170,
www.annagriffin.com

Botanical PaperWorks:
www.botanicalpaperworks.com

Camelot Wedding Stationery: 800-280-2860

Crane and Co.: 800-572-0024, www.crane.com

Evangel Christian Invitations: 800-457-9774,
   http://invitations.evangelwedding.com
Invitations by Dawn: 800-332-3296,
   www.invitationsbydawn.com
Julie Holcomb Printers: 510-654-6416,
   www.julieholcombprinters.com
Now and Forever: 800-451-8616,
   www.now-and-forever.com
PaperStyle.com (ordering invitations online):
   770-667-6100, www.paperstyle.com
Papyrus: www.papyrusonline.com
Precious Collection: 800-537-5222,
   www.preciouscollection.com
PSA Essentials: 248-288-7584,
   www.psaessentials.com
Renaissance Writings: 800-246-8483,
   www.RenaissanceWriting.com
Rexcraft: 800-635-3898, www.rexcraft.com
Willow Tree Lane: 800-219-9230,
   www.willowtreelane.com

Limousines

National Limousine Association: 800-NLA-7007,
   www.limo.org

Men's Wedding Wear

After Hours: www.afterhours.com
Gingiss: www.gingiss.com
Marrying Man: www.marryingman.com

Paper Products

OfficeMax: 800-283-7674, www.officemax.com
Paper Access: 800-727-3701, www.paperaccess.com
Paper Direct: 800-A-PAPERS, www.paperdirect.com
Staples: 800-333-3330, www.staples.com
The Wedding Store: www.wedguide.com/store
Ultimate Wedding Store:
    www.ultimatewedding.com/store
Wedmart.com: 888-802-2229, www.wedmart.com

Photo Albums

Exposures: 800-222-4947, www.exposuresonline.com

Rings

American Gem Society: 800-346-8485, www.ags.org
Benchmark: 800-633-5950,
    www.benchmarkrings.com
Bianca: 888-229-9229, www.BiancaCollection.com
Blue Nile: www.bluenile.com
Cartier: 800-CARTIER, www.cartier.com
Christian Bauer: 800-228-3724,
    www.christianbauer.com
DeBeers: www.adiamondisforever.com
EGL European Gemological Society: www.egl.co.za
Jeff Cooper Platinum: 888-522-6222,
    www.jeffcooper.com
Lazare Diamond: www.lazarediamonds.com
Novell: 888-916-6835, www.novelldesignstudio.com

OGI Wedding Bands Unlimited: 800-578-3846,
   www.ogi-ltd.com
Paul Klecka: www.klecka.com
Scott Kay Platinum: 800-487-4898,
   www.scottkay.com
Tiffany: 800-526-0649, www.tiffany.com
Wedding Ring Hotline: 800-985-RING,
   www.weddingringhotline.com
Zales: 800-311-JEWEL, www.zales.com
For information on how to design your own rings,
   check out www.adiamondisforever.com

Shoes and Handbags

Kenneth Cole: 800-KENCOLE,
   www.kennethcole.com
David's Bridal: 888-480-BRIDE
   www.davidsbridal.com
Dyeables: 800-431-2000, dyeables.com
Fenaroli for Regalia: 617-350-6556, www.fenaroli.com
Nina Footwear: www.ninashoes.com
Salon Shoes: 650-588-8677, www.salonshoes.com
Watters and Watters: 972-960-9884,
   www.watters.com

State and Location Tourism Departments

Tourism Office Worldwide Directory:

www.towd.com – This site will direct you to the most current and updated tourism department websites for any city in the United States and Canada, island, international destination, and tourist area. Through this all-inclusive site, you'll find tourism offices' special travel packages, free travel guide packages with promotional CD-ROMs, hotel links, things to do, historical FYIs and most popular attractions, seasonal specialties and further information for your smartest travel and wedding weekend research.

Veils and Headpieces

Bel Aire Bridals: 310-325-8160, www.belaireveils.com
David's Bridal: www.davidsbridal.com
Fenaroli for Regalia: 617-350-6556, www.fenaroli.com
Homa Creation: 973-467-5500, homabridal@aol.com
Reneé Romano: 312-943-0912,
    www.Renee-Romano.com
Winters & Rain: 401-848-0868,
    www.wintersandrain.com

Warehouse Stores

BJ's Wholesale Club: www.bjswholesale.com
Costco: www.costco.com
Sam's Club: www.samsclub.com

Weather Service and Sunsets

For checking the weather at your ceremony, reception, or honeymoon sites, including five-day forecasts and weather bulletins:

AccuWeather: www.accuweather.com

Sunset Time: (precise sunset time for any day of the year): http://aa.usno.navy.mil or www.sunrisesunset.com

Weather Channel: www.weather.com

Wedding Coordinators

Association of Bridal Consultants: 860-355-0464, www.bridalassn.com

Association of Certified Professional Wedding Consultants: 408-528-9000, www.acpwc.com

June Wedding Inc. (Consultants in the Western US): 702-474-9558, www.junewedding.com

Wedding Expert Associations

National Association of Catering Executives: www.nace.net

American Federation of Musicians: 212-869-1330

American Rental Association: 800-334-2177, www.ararental.org

American Society of Travel Agents: 703-739-2782, www.astanet.com

Professional Photographers of America: 800-786-6277, www.ppa-world.org

Wedding and Portrait Photographers International:
www.eventphotographers.com

Professional Videographer Association of America
(find your state's videography association):
209-653-8307, www.pva.com

American Disc Jockey Association: 301-705-5150,
www.adja.org

Wedding Items (Toasting Flutes, Ring Pillows, etc)

Affectionately Yours: www.affectionately-yours.com

Butterfly Celebration: 800-548-3284,
www.butterflycelebration.com

Chandler's Candle Company: 800-463-7143,
www.chandlerscandle.com

Keutbah Ketubah: 888-KETUBAH,
www.KETUBAH.com

Magical Beginnings Butterfly Farms: 888-639-9995,
www.butterflyevents.com (live butterflies for
release)

Michaels: 800-642-4235, www.michaels.com

The Wedding Shopper:
www.theweddingshopper.com/catalog.htm

Wedding Planning Websites

Sharon Naylor's Wedding Website:
www.SharonNaylor.net

Bliss Weddings: www.blissweddings.com

Bride's Magazine: www.brides.com

Della Weddings: www.della.com
Elegant Bride: www.elegantbride.com
Martha Stewart Living: www.marthastewart.com
Modern Bride: www.ModernBride.com
Premiere Bride: www.premierebride.com
The Best Man: www.thebestman.com
The Knot: www.theknot.com
The Wedding Channel: www.weddingchannel.com
Today's Bride: www.todaysbride.com
Town and Country Weddings (upscale):
    www.tncweddings.com
Wedding Bells: www.weddingbells.com

Wedding Registries

Bed Bath and Beyond: 800-GO-BEYOND,
    www.bedbathandbeyond.com
The Big Day (honeymoons): www.thebigday.com
Bloomingdales: 800-888-2WED,
    www.bloomingdales.com
Bon Ton: 800-9BONTON, www.bonton.com
Crate and Barrel: 800-967-6696,
    www.crateandbarrel.com
Dillards: 800-626-6001, www.dillards.com
Filene's: www.FilenesWeddings.com
Fortunoff: 800-777-2807, www.fortunoff.com
Gift Emporia.com: www.giftemporia.com
Gump's: www.gumps.com
Hecht's: www.hechts.com
Home Depot: www.homedepot.com
HoneyLuna (honeymoon registry): 800-809-5862